THE

QUARTERLY

EDITED BY

GORDON LISH

Readers will remember the surpassing example made present to us by the life of Hob Broun, taken by death two years ago this month. Two of the entries in Mr. Broun's last book, the collection of stories *Cardinal Numbers,* first appeared in *The Quarterly.* It is therefore with particular satisfaction that we note the award just received by *Cardinal Numbers* as the best work of fiction by an Oregon writer.

On the matter of so-called "multiple submissions,"
this magazine has not the slightest complaint with
whatever procedures might possibly speed the time
between a writer's deciding the work is ready for print
and print being achieved. If a writer elects to try a dozen
magazines at once in order to compress the time spent
on the grisly business of searching for a taker, then it would
seem such a writer is acting in accordance with good sense.
So far as *The Quarterly* is concerned, it is in the interest
of this magazine that those writers who choose to petition
for a place in its pages be in the most forgiving frame of
mind while doing the writing, while waiting for a response
to the writing, and—if this must be the outcome—while
receiving notification of the return of the writing.
If making "multiple submissions" can contribute, even
obliquely, to such a state of mind, then the entire estate
of writing profits—and, as a result, so does *The Quarterly.*
We therefore encourage the practice—on the notion that
what is good for writing cannot be bad for us.

THE
QUARTERLY

12 / WINTER 1989

VINTAGE BOOKS

A DIVISION OF RANDOM HOUSE, INC.

NEW YORK

The Quarterly (ISSN 0893-3103) is edited by Gordon Lish and is published March, June, September, and December for $36 the year ($48 in Canada) by Vintage Books, a division of Random House, Inc., 201 East 50th Street, New York, NY 10022. Application to mail at second-class postage rates is pending at New York, NY, and at additional mailing offices. Send orders and address changes to The Quarterly, Vintage Books, Subscription Department, Twenty-eighth Floor, 201 East 50th Street, New York, NY 10022. Back issues may be purchased, by check or money order, at $8.95 the copy; add $1.50 for postage and handling of each copy requested.

Management by Ellen F. Torron

The Quarterly welcomes the opportunity to read work of every character, and is especially concerned to keep itself an open forum. Manuscripts must be accompanied by the customary return materials, and should be addressed to The Editor, The Quarterly, 201 East 50th Street, New York, NY 10022. The Quarterly makes the utmost effort to offer its response to manuscripts no later than one week subsequent to receipt. Opinions expressed herein are not necessarily those of the editor or of the publisher.

isbn: 0-679-72153-3

Design by Andrew Roberts
Installation by Denise Stewart

Some issues ago the editor made a statement of his indebtedness to a number of persons whose interventions are crucial to the life of this magazine but whose names are not shown herein. Then there is the case of Ellen F. Torron, whose name will appear herein for as long as there is a herein for her name to appear in, even should she take herself away from this magazine as far as she can get. To be sure, there never would have been a herein if Ellen F. Torron had not been. Live forever! Ellen F. Torron— but, hey, when you feel yourself failing, tell us what the F. stands for.

Manufactured in the United States of America

THE QUARTERLY

THE
QUARTERLY

Her husband died

© 89

Duchesne

In Duchesne these things happen.

Children run wild.

Spence and Tina sit in the burnt-out Texaco and take drags on their Camels. Night is falling on them like a dark parent and they are caught with their faces pale. It is past time to go home and here they are, letting go of their evenings.

Tina lets the smoke run from her mouth like a fluid.

"I've been diddled," Tina says. She is twelve and talking about the grocery boy that laid her behind the market.

Spence pops his jaw and blows smoke. His complexion is so clear. He knew that grocery boy.

"You don't believe me, do you, Spence?" Tina asks. She rides her sweater up.

Spence feels her tummy.

Tina has taken to wearing barrettes. She clips them on instead of combing. Hygiene has lost all meaning.

"Yeah, I felt it," Spence says.

Tina's just puffing out her stomach. She has the cheeks of a squirrel and the breasts of a mother, but she isn't pregnant.

Spence is sitting on a cinderblock that has fallen from the Texaco's walls. The cold rises around him. On the highway, a truck is making the long haul to Salt Lake. They feel the vibrations of its passing, these two children who should be home by now.

"Can you feel a pulse?" Spence asks. He puts his two fingers on her wrist.

Tina pulls his hand back to her belly.

"It's in here," she says.

Spence's hand is cold. November is almost over. A herd of crows hang above the Texaco.

"Can you feel the beating of its heart?" Tina asks.

"It must be very small," Spence says. His hand is on her, but it is the noise of a baby that he listens for.

"A walnut," Tina says.

Tina is a ghost with her arms raised. Her shirt is almost off, the cigarette always caught there between her lips.

"Come home," Spence says. He is urgently gathering his cigarettes and his books.

"I'll ride my bike," says Tina.

By dinnertime, she has not arrived.

Tina has climbed the walls of the Texaco and is standing like a bird on the narrow cinderblocks.

Duchesne mothers should worry about their children. Duchesne mothers stay up late. They wake their husbands at three.

They say, "Our children have no table manners."

They say, "Children should speak when children are spoken to."

"The girls sit like men," they say in Duchesne, this unsheltered Utah town. In Wyoming, children are taught these things in school.

Rumor has it, and most agree, that there might be werewolves here. Women sit in the laundromat and talk about the droppings werewolves leave.

Werewolves steal the garbage and their eyebrows grow together.

The smell of meat is everywhere.

They live on ranches.

Spence and Tina's mother knows these things, and still she lets her children wander the neighborhood after dark.

She should warn them that moons have nothing to do with it. Not one little thing at all

Returning from the Texaco, Spence and Tina pass all the dark cornfields. They stand on the edge. They gather stones and chuck them in high arcs.

Spence sends his rocks like artillery into the corn.

"After high school, maybe I could be a nurse," Tina says.

"People need janitors too, or people to wash their dishes."

"People should wash their own dishes," says Tina.

"Do you want a cigarette?" Spence asks.

Spence lights it for her, cupping the lit match with his hand and drawing sharply. Tina is swinging her arm in the dark.

Water congeals in the town's fields.

Behind a neighbor's barn, coyotes have circled a cow with their yapping jaws and brought it to its knees.

Spence can't sleep. Downstairs, the noise of his mother's feet fills the house.

Tina's window is open, and outside, the moon is curved and sharp like a woman's chin. Tina is asleep. Her nightgown is twisted. The covers have been thrown to the floor.

Spence goes to her, feeling for her belly.

"Tina," he whispers.

He says, "Tina, do you hear mother?"

"Maybe she's mending. Does she have the fire going?" Tina asks.

Spence says, "She is in the parlor, then she goes to the kitchen, then she comes back again."

They spread the blankets over them and he closes his eyes.

"Spence," Tina says.

She takes hold of her brother's arm, but he has fallen asleep so fast.

Tina rides her bike all over Duchesne. She stops at the feed store to smile at farmers. They sit like hicks. They carry bags on their shoulders. They try to place her. Does she live out with the Taylors? Tina grips her handlebars and the men get into their trucks and drive away.

Tina's bicycle has three speeds. She leans into curves.

It is like Spence is running behind her. **Q**

J. R. RODRIGUEZ

Unravelling

I took Frankie Nebo out with a left to the temple that would have stopped a train. John Ventura ate canvas after a trio of right hooks took off his insipid face. I stopped Spider Cusack—*there* was a jaw—with a straight left to the solar plexus—heard him bite right through his mouthpiece.

Gate receipts, weights, crowd totals stick in my head. My cornerman, Duns Scotus Himplemman, is dead. Gyms depress me—always have. The civic center in Oklahoma City doesn't, it has big glass walls. I like to look down a main street from inside.

Something is wrong. My hands hurt all the time and I, and I alone, sing my song.

Next door the Rivera girls dance. They work in a supermarket and bring me Johnny Walker Black at cost and mangos—super ripe, sticking together and smelling of incense. They are fifteen and sixteen, Diana and Penelope. The only way to tell them apart is by their breasts, which are large. The disparity is in the shape: Di round, Penny angled and sharp. Their mother works all the time. The girls come over. I help them with their homework. Penny eats numbers and geometric proofs—makes up problems to kill time—and they fry up bananas and pork chops. I got them opera tickets last year, and now Di comes over to play her cello.

They come over and we watch a ball game.

"There are so many ugly people in New York," Penny says.

"Don't you ever miss Oklahoma?" she asks me.

"Yeah, but not too bad," I say.

"Did you ever see Clemente play?" Di asks.

"Sure," I say. "I met him once."

"Really?" they say.

"Yes." I look out the window.

"It's ugly, huh?"

I don't say anything. We stand there until the inning ends.

Sometimes I see Siegfried, big chest and thick arms. He has burns on his body but knows that he is alive and fucking triumphant. He is holding Brünnhilde and, behind him, a fire burns, but he is oblivious to it. The Valkyries stare at him, amazed at his courage and prowess, waving and singing to him.

They are happy.

They cry.

There were times—early in the morning, during dinner, didn't matter—when I was on, really on, pure electric dismantling power, kids and women would get all red and I was a river, blue neon flowing—you'd jump in if you could.

I was beautiful then.

A hundred sixty pounds.

It wasn't that long ago. River run.

When Duns Scotus Himpelmman died, I was in Port Lyndsay. I drove into Wales about five in the morning, my mouth glued shut by something that had once been ale—my mind amazed at how pale white Scottish girls were undressed—and still hoping that through some magnificent primordial warrior trait I would wake up in London.

This guy Colin—damn, I like that name—was behind the bar when I found out where I was.

"You teaching?" he says.

"Tourist," I say.

"Good," he says. "Seen Chartres?"

"No."

"Don't bother. It's a mess, cut and simple."

"Thanks," I say.

"You Yank-Irish?" Colin says.

"Yeah."

"Better than Irish-Irish," he says. "Pigs. Stupid as the day has minutes. Look at their dogs. Can't train them. Got sheep running all over the place. Aaagh. You know Gene Vincent?" he says.

"Sure," I say.

"What's the flip side of 'Be Bop a Lula'?"

It goes: She's been waiting all the morning long . . .

"That's it," Colin says. "What's it called?"

"I don't know."

Colin and I think about it all day.

At my hotel, the desk clerk looks depressed. "A wire for you, sir." He gives it to me.

It says my cornerman is dead.

"It's okay," I say.

In the hotel bar that night I tap my glass and try to remember what Colin and I were talking about.

Duns saw me in Union City one time. I was thirteen, I go one thirty-nine and am still fighting righty. I move in with him and his mom, sleeping in the kitchen when it's cold. He gets me a pair of shoes. I sell the ones I'd stolen.

"You got to know what's real," he always said. I never knew what he was talking about, but after he switched me back to southpaw, made me move my left foot forward, and got me to eat, I was a machine, couldn't get a fight—even in Philly—and I was, for more than a while, a fucking God.

I could tag—who couldn't?—but what I did better than anyone else, anyone ever, was find the mark. Slightly off center of chin, behind the ear, it was like a blinking Christmas light, glowing, wanting to be tapped and broken. I could see it in total dead blackness. The thing was this: lights start to blink everywhere, all the time and—snap—just like that, it's gone.

"Everyone is a dicksmack," Penny says.

Di nods her head. When she takes a break from her cello, she rubs her bow on her head. There is resin and white horsehair on her brown clump. She points to Penny's leg with her bow. "Strong. Killer-strong. Lean, pray for prey, you could really survive on those legs."

"Dancer's legs," Penny says.

"Not just. More. Their explosiveness redeems." Di taps Penny's head with her bow.

I cut mango strips and put them in a dish with J-Dub Black. The girls take pieces.

"God, I'm happy," Di says.

I cut seventeen pounds in four days to make weight once. By the fifth round, the tape on my gloves kept unravelling and I couldn't pick my arms up.

"Sweat," Duns told me. "That's not really you in that ring."

"That's right," I said. "I'm not really here. I left my life in a sauna yesterday."

"This is real," Duns said, taping me up and giving me my mouthpiece. To me the man looked old. "You want me to cut your gloves off?" Duns said.

"No," I said. I smiled, slumped in my small corner, no Christmas light to look forward to, my life cut and sprawled into three-minute pieces.

A little while later the ref asked me what city I was in.

"Helena," I said. "And damned beautiful it is, all kudzu-covered the way it is in spring."

"Helena is a fucking hickpit hole," Duns yelled.

"Yes, yes," I said. "Quite right. I'm thinking of the North-west Territories—before the gold rush, of course."

I no longer live three minutes at a time.

I'm in a bar looking out at the Met. There's a fight on the television. It's the last night of Wagner. Across the street there's this girl. I met her one night before I had a bit at the Garden.

She looks the same.

She's wearing a suit.

Nice.

She was at Columbia Law then. Her name was Britmore. She wore a pretty white dress that night. It was summer. I'd made weight by a pound and a half. I was a fucking, freaking, goddamn gladiator-king, she said. **Q**

Smoke

The Timmonses stood facing Harry on Harry's porch. Harry stood in his doorway. He was wishing he hadn't answered their knock without his shirt. It felt funny to him, standing there without a shirt. He thought maybe Mr. Timmons felt the same way. There was a look in Mr. Timmons's eye. It really was funny—because Harry and the Timmonses had never met.

"We're the Timmonses," Mrs. Timmons had said, and then one thing led to another until she was holding Mr. Timmons's elbow and saying, "Well, then, just don't call it a divorce ranch, honey."

"What else do you expect me to call it?" said Mr. Timmons, "when that's what it is? Do you expect if I call it something else it'll be different, or what? It seems funny, is all, a divorce ranch. I hope it's worth it to you, living out here."

"Oh, it is," said Mrs. Timmons. "It's lovely out here."

Harry kept his arms folded over his chest and tried not looking at the Timmonses, who had just moved into the cottage across the courtyard, number three. Separated by the clothesline and the little stretch of lawn, number three was no different from Harry's cottage. Harry knew that because he had snuck through number three when the last people had moved out. It was just like his was, only empty. He had wondered who would move in and what kind of things they would have and whether they would be the kind of people who have plants. And now here they were, on his porch, the Timmonses.

Harry figured he already knew some things about the Timmonses. He had watched them from his window as they hauled in boxes, tables, chairs from the U-Haul. It looked to him the way it always looked, the moving and the stuff being moved. It was young stuff. First-marriage stuff. Harry knew which of the stuff was Mr. Timmons's and which was Mrs. Timmons's.

He knew they would have to take the bed apart to get it through the door. What he didn't know was whether the Timmonses were the kind of people to go and get plants.

Harry had thought about helping.

He scratched his chest and felt his navel for lint.

"Don't you think so, Drake?" Mr. Timmons was saying.

"What?" said Harry.

"Don't you think it's funny, living on an old divorce ranch?" Mr. Timmons said.

Harry hooked his thumbs in his pockets and stared at his naked feet.

That was in April.

Mrs. Timmons started doing Harry's wash in May. It was after the time a pair of red socks turned his white things pink. She caught him in the laundry room holding up his sheet to the light and when he told her no, these sheets were not supposed to be pink, Mrs. Timmons said: "I'll tell you what, how would you like for me to do your wash? Really," said Mrs. Timmons. "It's no trouble. It's part of why I, we, moved out here. I never really got a sense of neighbors, living there in town. Honest, it's no trouble. You work," she said. "You're a bachelor. You could probably do me a favor someday. I wash Mondays."

Mrs. Timmons took the sheet from Harry.

"Besides," she said, "I just can't see a fella like you sleeping on pink."

In July, it began hitting over a hundred out and Harry lost his job. At first it wasn't so bad. He kept busy with unemployment papers, television, bologna logs, and five-pound bricks of government cheddar. He slept until noon and carried the fan with him wherever he went—bathroom, living room, kitchen. There was no reason to go out, and he didn't.

"This is the life," he said to himself. "Beats hell out of banging nails."

He thought he could go on eating bologna, cheddar, and ketchup sandwiches forever, and there was a little girl on *Days of Our Lives* he lived to see get corked. Every day he woke up, carried the fan into the living room, rubbed his hands together, and said:

"See if she gets corked today."

He was surprised at the way he felt. He took it personally. She was a tease. Harry thought about it. A tease. He felt he knew a tease when he saw one.

He sat still on the sofa watching. The fan air moved his hair. His stomach begged for bologna and cheddar. But only the sound of a tire iron outside got him up.

He saw Mrs. Timmons changing a flat tire. But he heard his stomach, and went to the kitchen to make a sandwich.

He spent the day and the night watching television in front of the fan. He thought he might be getting a stomachache. He blamed the bologna. Too much of a good thing. Maybe tomorrow, he thought, he could doctor it with Top Ramen.

He switched off the television, dragged his fan to the bathroom, washed his armpits, brushed his teeth.

It was then he learned, if he put his ear to it, he could hear what the Timmonses were saying from number three.

"Poor man, my ass!" he heard Mr. Timmons yelling. "The lousy son-of-a-bitch doesn't work! Hell with that neighbor garbage! He can do his own wash!"

Harry turned off the fan. There was a waiting sort of no sound for a while and then he heard Mrs. Timmons say:

"Well, he changed a tire for me today."

Sweat beaded on Harry's forehead.

Next day Harry cleaned house. He dragged the fan into the kitchen and started in with the vacuum. He vacuumed over the open part of the floor twice. He moved the table and chairs and vacuumed until the foot impressions were sucked up flat. With the nozzle attachment he vacuumed in the space between the stove and the cupboards, vacuumed cobwebs out of corners, vacuumed dust and dead flies from windowsills. He moved the fan into the bathroom, then into the bedroom, vacuuming around the mirror, along the base of the tub, under the bed, behind the dresser. He filled an entire bag and then he was finished. He threw the bag away, closed his eyes, and put his face up close to the fan on the kitchen table.

It was surprising to him what he had been living with.

He opened the refrigerator and pulled out the bologna and the cheddar. Then he remembered his stomach. He turned on the television. But it was Saturday and there was nothing on he really wanted to watch.

He decided to shave and take a shower.

He shaved carefully, making sure to catch even the whiskers under his nose and on his neck. He splashed water on his face and checked closely, seeing how the fan moved the soapy water across his chin. Then he stepped into the shower. He soaped, scrubbed, rinsed, and did it all again. Behind his ears, in his ass, the bottoms of his feet. He washed his hair. The water felt good. He tried touching his toes. He straightened up and reached his hands to the ceiling. He parted the curtains, wiped the water from the window, saw Mr. Timmons across the courtyard lighting a barbecue.

Mrs. Timmons stood behind Mr. Timmons. Harry saw her look up and see him in the window. He was almost sure of it. He saw goose pimples on his arms and legs. He shuddered when he moved closer to the fan and rolled the Speed Stick under his arms. The mirror told him he was ready. He could never be readier.

"I'm ready," he said, and the sound of his voice startled him. He said it again, his lips right up against the fan. "I'm ready," he said.

The smell of chicken teriyaki made its way across the courtyard and through his window and mixed in the fan air with the smell of shrimp Ramen. Harry cut a thick slab off the cold bologna log and slapped it in a frying pan. The bologna spat and sizzled in the pan and when the singed edges curled, Harry forked the meat and flipped it over. The bologna was quiet until he pressed down where the center stood up from the pan. When it was just right, he forked the meat onto a plate and poured the Ramen on it. He carried the plate to the table, and then dragged the fan over. He fetched a napkin from the cupboard and a knife from the drawer. He checked his window. Mrs. Timmons was there, under her porch light, holding the plate of chicken teriyaki. He didn't see her go back into her place, but saw her standing there, looking at his door.

Harry moved from the window. He held his breath. Then he hurried, clearing pots and pans from the stove, his plate from the table, putting everything into the refrigerator. He unplugged the fan, carried it to the living room, and sat on the sofa and waited. He waited until he decided she was not going to come.

He carried the fan back into the kitchen and opened the refrigerator and saw the Ramen and bologna under the bright bulb. It hadn't seemed so gray. He stuck his finger in it.

Brick cold.

He left it there and closed the refrigerator.

He heard laughter, her laughter, Mrs. Timmons's laughter. He switched the fan to low and he heard through Mrs. Timmons's laughter Mr. Timmons's voice.

Harry pulled a chair up to the window. He listened awhile and then he turned off all his lights.

He could see their shapes. He saw them at their table behind the window shade. He watched. He saw her feed him with her hand. He saw Timmons shake his head and heard him growl like a dog. He heard Mrs. Timmons laugh again, saw her throw up her hands, lean back in her chair while Mr. Timmons raised a glass to his lips. Mrs. Timmons stood and reached a glass out to Mr. Timmons.

He saw Mrs. Timmons's shadow go away.

Nothing happened for a time except some talking Harry couldn't hear through the fan. He tried switching the fan off, but it got too hot. Mr. Timmons might be smoking, Harry thought.

Finally, he saw her come back again.

Then the kitchen light went out.

Harry put his elbows on his knees and his forehead in his hands. He closed his eyes, opened them, then closed them again. He straightened up and filled his lungs with air. He tilted his head back and let the air out.

His chest ached.

Across the courtyard, he saw the bathroom light come on. Then the bedroom.

He took the fan into his bedroom, switched it on high, and took his clothes off. On his knees, on his bed, he watched.

A shape appeared behind the bedroom shade—Mrs. Timmons's.

Harry leaned forward, his hands on the windowsill. The shade went up, and there was Mrs. Timmons getting her blouse off.

Then the bathroom light went off and the window shade came down.

It got quiet.

Harry leaned forward again, put his ear to the screen.

He shut the fan off.

He stood up on his bed, trying to get a better angle, but it was like trying to look up a skirt on TV.

He suddenly thought he heard Mr. Timmons say "Honey." Harry thought he heard Mr. Timmons say that—say "Honey."

He jerked off. He wiped it off with his sheet. He turned on the fan.

There was nothing left to vacuum. He didn't need a shave. He kept an eye out over the clothesline and the lawn and he listened. He thought he would maybe put out his eyes and ears, or move in to town.

When Monday morning came, Harry found himself in bed, peering out his window while Mr. Timmons started his car and left for work. Harry got up, pissed, carried the fan to the living room. He watched the morning news, learned the high for the day would be 105, thought how bad the plans you make late at night seem by the light of day.

All in all, he felt pretty good.

He made a new plan.

First, he got his dirty clothes, towels, sheets, into the laundry basket. Next, he wrote a note saying he was sick and could Mrs. Timmons please just take these things and leave them when she was finished. He set the basket and the note on his porch, stared out his window, then closed all the curtains and turned the volume up on the TV.

Then he climbed out of the sofa to go find something to eat. He carried the fan to the kitchen and began searching the cupboards. He found lime Jell-O.

"Okay," he said.

He mixed the Jell-O and put it in the refrigerator and unplugged the fan. He started for the living room, then went to look through the curtain to check on his laundry. The basket was gone.

The game shows were on. Then it was time for *Days of Our Lives.* He watched a while, then hurried to inspect the Jell-O. He put his finger in it. He heard Mrs. Timmons in the courtyard. He closed the refrigerator. He parted the curtains over the sink. She was out there, wearing a bathing suit, hanging the wash to dry. Harry noticed the way the elastic crept up her buttocks when she reached to hang something. He saw there was nothing so wonderful about her body.

He went back.

The boyfriend had his hands on her shoulders. The girl was telling him she didn't know, she wasn't sure, didn't think she was old enough, didn't think it was right. Did he love her? If he loved her, he would understand.

"Understand, shit," said Harry, "poor guy just wants a shot at the bearded clam."

He turned off the TV, carried the fan to the kitchen, parted the curtains over the sink. Harry saw how Mrs. Timmons hadn't done anything about her elastic, how it had crept up even farther. He saw how she was halfway through hanging things. He let the curtains fall back, took the Jell-O from the refrigerator, a knife from the drawer. He cut a square in the Jell-O and tried lifting it with the knife. The Jell-O spread all around the knife. The knife did not lift anything up.

He tried a spoon. He gave it up and went to get his mirror sunglasses.

The heat outside went into his lungs. Even the sunglasses could not cut the glare. He steadied himself on the porch railing.

"Holy smokes," he said.

Mrs. Timmons turned at his voice. She smiled. He saw that there were spots on the suit below her breasts and at her navel.

"Feeling better?" she said.

"Little," Harry said.

"Summer cold?" she said.

"Stomach thing," Harry said.

She did not fix her elastic.

"Flu?" she said. "My husband says there's a bug going around town."

Harry left his porch, went toward her.

"No," Harry said. "Think it might be bologna. Been eating a lot of bologna."

"Bologna?" said Mrs. Timmons. "Is that all you eat?"

"That and cheddar. Bologna and cheddar. And Top Ramen. You can doctor it up some with Top Ramen and it's okay," Harry said.

Mrs. Timmons kept squeezing a clothespin open and shut.

"Sounds awful," she said. "Bologna. A man can't live on bologna and Ramen. You better have lunch with me. Leftover chicken. We barbecued it the other night, teriyaki."

Harry didn't say anything. Mrs. Timmons turned back to the clothesline. The elastic had crept halfway up. He thought how that must feel.

"You want a hand?" he said.

"Well, sure," Mrs. Timmons said. "Pins are in that coffee can. You just go help yourself."

He grabbed a handful of clothespins. He took a towel and a shirt. He picked up a pair of his pants. Sweat stung his eyes and blurred his vision. He blinked, and it was when he blinked that the clothespin snapped closed, catching the loose part of some skin just right.

He dropped the pants, shook his finger, said: "Sonofabitch!"

"Oh," said Mrs. Timmons, "you all right?"

Harry took his finger from his mouth. There was a blood blister there.

"Boy, that smarts," he said.

Mrs. Timmons came close, put her hands on either side of his hand, but did not touch his hand. She pouted and looked into Harry's sunglasses.

"Let me hang these last few things," she said, "and then I'll take you into the house and see if we can't make it feel better."

Harry did not take off the sunglasses inside. He left them on and through them he saw everything he had already seen when they had moved in. The table, the chairs, the lamp with the lace frills. The clock set in lacquered redwood hung on the wall, and the free-standing bookcase held the unboxed photographs, pots, pans.

Mrs. Timmons bent to take the chicken teriyaki from the refrigerator. Harry watched her bend. She put the stuff on the table. She looked Harry's way, then dumped the ashtray in the garbage under the sink and said:

"Disgusting habit he has. Do you smoke?"

"Sometimes," said Harry.

"Drink?"

"Not now."

"Come on back to the bedroom," she said. "I've got some needles there that should do the trick for that blister."

"Needles?" said Harry.

"To relieve the pressure," said Mrs. Timmons.

Harry followed her. He followed her through the living room, past the bathroom, into the bedroom. He felt the difference, seeing the rooms and the furniture in the rooms, now that they were together and the people used them.

"I usually just leave them alone till they go away," he said.

"Don't be silly," she said.

In the bedroom, standing at the foot of the bed, he looked from their window across the courtyard to the closed curtained reflection of his own windows. He watched Mrs. Timmons searching drawers for a needle to relieve the pressure.

"Voila!" she said, and straightened up, looking, Harry thought, right through his sunglasses.

"Will it be safe?" Harry said.

"Safe?" said Mrs. Timmons.

"I mean, will I get an infection?"

"Oh, I doubt it," said Mrs. Timmons. "But I'll sterilize it if you like."

Harry saw her pick up a lighter from the top of the bureau and hold the flame to the needle. He wiped the sweat from his forehead with the back of his arm.

"You'll be careful?" he said.

"Of course," she said. "Don't be such a baby. Now," she said, and reached for Harry's hand.

"Just be careful," he said.

She took his hand in hers, trying to steady his finger. She

touched the needle to the purple blister. Harry thought he could see his pulse in the blister.

"Relax," she said.

Harry took a deep breath and held it. He turned his head from his finger. He looked again at the bed and again out the window and then he said, "Did you see me in the shower?"

"Yes," she said.

She stuck him.

She stuck him and he flinched and the needle drove into the meat of his finger. Blood spread out from the blister.

He tried to pull his hand back. He felt himself trying to pull his hand back.

But she wouldn't let go.

She held him.

"There's more," she said, and stuck him again. **Q**

Salmon

The wife: standing at sink, all done up, plucking bones out of salmon with tweezers, sliding knife between fat and sticky layer, sticking knife under running water, sink full of papery scales and soggy skin. Few flakes of scale fall to the floor, stick to silk pouf at the toe of her shoe, to shoe itself, a watery marshland print, a pump with a tapered heel and toe, a walking shoe for dressy trips.

The husband: cutting board set up, small knife and large knife laid out, checking freezer, jerking door open, shoving door shut when it is made to snuff itself shut.

Limes? he says.

Her chin is the way he can tell, if watching; if yes, nodding. But is not watching her chin, muffled with her neck in some airy, floating thing. A neckerchief? Butterflies on it, as if he noticed—not moths, if he supposed. A bumblebee pin pinned to the pad attached to her shoulder. Flying things, if anything—if he looked.

We didn't have to invite them, he says. We could have uninvited them.

Wife is rinsing drainboard with flexible hose, papery scales that are not rinsing off, wiping at them with paper toweling which they anyway stick to, not nodding, the butterflies not seeming to flutter into anything, her neckerchief.

What did you do with the pitcher? he says, as if she had done something to it, had nicked one of its facets, had lent it.

Wife points to closet with dripping hand, puts hand back under faucet, rubs at scales stuck to palms, pinches thinner needle-like bones stuck to fingers, the few more jutting hair-like from the fillet, pinches and plucks.

So! the sangria, husband says, unscrewing the cap from

the jug with the rapid motion wife thinks of when wife thinks of him, her rapid husband.

One lime he rapidly halves. The other he slices. The slices fall rapidly beneath the small knife.

Blood oranges, husband says.

Wife points to sack on floor. Husband moves rapidly to spill them out of sack onto cutting board, to split with large knife, to set them with their mottled sides up.

Wife is wiping up red juice, rinsing sponge under faucet, taking up lime slice, rubbing it pointlessly across palm, pinching up coarse salt from salt cellar, rubbing palm to remove sea smell, smelling palm.

Done, husband says, handing wife the small knife to run under running water, wiping hands on the cloth tucked into belt.

Wife furnishes husband with avocado, tomato, scallions, cilantro. Wife wraps fish, each fillet, in plastic wrap wrapped with a sprig of cilantro. Wife takes up sponge and wipes floor, gets up bits of skin, peel, droppings, drops of water.

Husband is rapidly skinning tomato.

If you really do not like them, husband says, we can drop them.

Husband has chopped avocado, scallions, cilantro, is taking ice chips from freezer and is dropping them into bowl. Wife is hosing down drainboard, sidestepping splashes that splash down, splashing shoes, poufs, watery marshlands.

Maybe I should have left my shoes in the closet, wife is thinking, maybe I should go barefoot.

He is a good one to know, though, husband says, though you never know.

Payback is payback, wife says, blotting shoes.

Neckerchief, if he looked, is seeming to flutter. Wife is seeming to bend back her back. Wife is thinking: They are hatched; they are making their way from downstream to upstream, where they will leap up.

I don't know about her, though, husband says.

Wife is thinking: My watery shoes should come off. She is taking them off if he looked; she is hosing her feet; she is wrapping them; she is dressing them up. Wife thinks of them at the rapids, one of them walking rapidly, the other, changing altitude, leisurely, unrapidly leaping up. **Q**

Desire

Collins is locked in the antechamber of the night vault, where it is cool, or at least cooler than it is in the rest of the building. The air conditioning shut down automatically hours ago. It must be 85 degrees in here, 90 maybe, and the air is as still as stone. There are no fans in banks. They play havoc with loose bills.

The bank is hot and empty and I do not feel safe. I'm not concerned about Collins. Even if the vault is air-tight, which I doubt, he should have plenty of oxygen, particularly if he has the brains to lie down. I'll mention it to him later.

It's not Collins that makes me anxious, nor the stack of bills on his desk, more than three thousand dollars. No, it's being here, in a bank, that puts me on edge. Something about it makes me want to slide a chair beneath the door handle. I feel frail and vulnerable in banks—not a helpful attitude to have as a bank manager.

No wonder I have difficulty inspiring the confidence of my depositors. I start at small noises. Nictitating behind my desk, I am alarmed by the gentle, hydraulic sucking noise of the front door opening and closing. From the officers' enclosure, I look up when I hear the door, and I see shadows racing across the floor and hurdling into the tellers' cage, or into the vault. There is too much desire in the world, and too little money, to feel entirely safe in a bank.

For safety, at least, I envy Collins his cool steel cocoon. Not likely any harm will come to him in there. For me there is nothing but heat, and no hope of respite until the sun passes behind the peaked roof of the pharmacy across the town square.

I must stay in the hot, shadowy recesses until the stores close and the sidewalks and parking spaces empty.

. . .

Collins is only my most recent mistake. Fat and sloppy, his glasses riding down his nose as his shirttails ride up and out of his pants, allowing the view (if you want it) of the sweaty place where his back cleaves into two before being swallowed up by his rubbery underwear . . . Well, I never should have hired him, but he passed the aptitude test in the main office in Stamford, and delicately called me "Sir" in our interview, so I forgave the moisture he left in my hand when we shook afterward. If I could find something he would be good at, if I could steer him somewhere else, I would fire him. I should have done it long ago. His single virtue is punctuality, which doesn't get you far.

This afternoon he came up three thousand dollars long. Three thousand, one hundred and thirty, exactly. If only he had come up short! Short means the bank is out a few bucks. But long is a sticky situation. Long means somebody (a widow, no doubt) expects that money to show up on her balance. It means we have stolen from an unwitting depositor. Long puts your ass in a sling.

"I just don't know where it could be," he told me sweatily, long after everyone else had totaled up and gone home. We dumped his trash can and sifted through it, studying each slip of paper for a clue. We dug through his drawer, searching for a missing deposit receipt. We rang up his credits and debits, added and subtracted their sums, checked and rechecked the figures, and all the while he murmured apologies and cleared his throat softly.

Finally the heat got to me and I locked him up. He was as obedient as an old Labrador when I requested that he go into the vault. I escorted him in, holding him lightly under his left arm, feeling the damp cloth of his sleeve between my thumb and finger. He stood in the middle of the chamber and watched impassively as I shut and latched the light metal grill from the outside, but the blood drained from his face when I put my shoulder to the outer door, a ton of reinforced steel that, with a little prodding, swings as smoothly as a golf club.

I heard a catch in his throat as the door shut. But he didn't sob or whimper or beg me to reconsider. "Procedure," I called through the steel.

Being a small-town banker isn't what it once was. These days, money is cast into the sea. My depositors picture themselves cattle barons on the plains of Brazil, numismatists, stock-market wizards, real-estate geniuses. They don't put their money in banks anymore.

Their financial dabbling has rendered my career meaningless. My services are of no importance. Once, I counseled caution; now I say to hell with it, put your money wherever you please! I've done the same with my own.

Jennie points out interesting investments. I own a piece of timberland in Maine that I have never seen. I backed a polymer scientist who was working up a new material for soft contact lenses. He eventually took a job with Du Pont, though he still sends a card at Christmas. I plunked down a few grand to help develop a new artificial sweetener, and did the same when I learned about a small company that wanted to make a vitamin A cough syrup.

Not a little accomplishment for a man still in his thirties! But I don't ask for recognition—just a return on investment. I'm behind on both cars, the house—Jesus, the house— Bloomingdale's and Macy's. I'm being dunned by Jennie's gynecologist and my own dentist. I've had to renege on a pledge of two thousand for a new library in town.

But money counts for nothing in heaven. I'll stand before him at the gates, and I'll turn my pockets inside out. I'll point down to my adoration for Jennie, my place in the community, my healthy attitude toward PRs and Jews. I'll get by.

I have no desire for money. As an experiment, I once burned the cash in my wallet, testing its connection to me, probing myself to see if I felt loss. It was Sunday morning. Jennie was at the market, getting doughnuts for breakfast. The kids were watching television. The sprinkler was on in the back yard, fanning the lawn with water, spattering the patio, where I found some twigs and dry leaves for kindling. I made a little pile on the bricks and draped the cash on top of it. I don't remember how much, but there was a twenty there, a ten certainly, probably forty bucks in all. I touched a match to a bit of dry moss poking from under the corner of a bill. It smoked, ignited, and in a moment the whole pile was consumed by flames.

I felt nothing.

The money had nothing to do with me.

I fear I'm going to take a fall on the antiques market. It's Jennie's latest passion. She is not acquisitive, but impulsive. She keeps a stack of Sotheby's catalogues by the kitchen phone, and I have seen her poring over them like a scholar, twirling a knot of blond hair around her finger as she turns the heavy pages.

We have made only one major purchase. Call it an investment. A harp, a monstrous thing caked with flaking gold leaf. Somehow this hulk maintains an incongruous essence of daintiness, like a fly's wing.

We found it in the window of a Greenwich Village antique shop. "My God, Mark" is what Jennie said, and for a moment I didn't know why she was alarmed.

She pointed to the window. "You don't know how to play the harp," I said, knowing suddenly that she wanted it.

"It's just the most beautiful thing I've ever seen."

I became tangled in the interconnectedness of things. I conceived invisible strands tying me to far-off persons and places. I imagined the artists, actual harpists, who might appreciate the instrument, who might actually need such a thing as a harp. "Think of all the people who need a harp more than we do," I said.

"I'm thinking of it in the living room right now," she said.

She doesn't understand the endless ripples that issue from our wake. The dynamics of economics, the dialectic of supply and demand. I considered pointing out that, by purchasing the harp, the price of everything connected with it would rise, simply because we had lessened supply. Harp strings, harp lessons, concerts, even tea at the Ritz, where the harps sing like angels each afternoon at four! Or so I have been led to believe.

Now the harp bides its time unplayed in a corner of the living room. Late at night, the cat rubs its back against the instrument's strings and I sit up in bed, spooked by the strange soft dissonance.

Some days, sitting at my desk, I spot Jennie crossing the town square to the supermarket. I have come to understand that she is the last of her kind, a dinosaur. There are no more suburban housewives, as charming as the breed may have been long ago. No one but Czechs play tennis anymore.

But she could go to law school! Hell, yes, why not? I can see Jennie studiously taking notes in a lecture hall. I can picture her an associate (hell, a partner!) in a stodgy law firm, buttoned down in flannel and silk.

Jennie wears light cotton dresses in warm weather, and even from the distance, watching her from my desk, divided as we are by the bank floor, the olive-tinted windows, the sidewalk leading to the supermarket, I can make out the gentle definition of the muscles in her calves. Her bare shoulders are smooth. They slope gradually into her arms, which are unnaturally long.

But she can stagger me.

I came home one evening not long ago to find that her hair was suddenly curly, exploding around her face, where it once tucked neatly behind her ears and draped straight to her shoulders. It was as if she had presented a new self to me.

Bigamist, I rushed her to the bedroom before she could

ask if I liked the new style. I sniffed at her neck, inhaled the residue of hairdresser's tonics and the sickly sweet odor of talc.

There was no time for diaphragm; Jennie was caught up in the excitement of the new as well. Watching me watch her, she tugged at a sprig of curl as I chucked my clothes on the floor, pulled my shirt—half-buttoned, tie still threaded through the collar—over my head. I fell onto the bed and paused to listen (for what? a child's cry? footsteps on the driveway?) before she grabbed me. I pinned her arms over her head, intoxicated by newness.

And that evening, I learned that the new Jennie was still the old. The permanent cost $175, she said, her back to me as she worked at the stove. I thought: I am beholden to a queen hairdresser in Westport. The interconnectedness is ever more clear. The web expands. I am a contributor, no doubt, to a condominium development in Key West.

Jennie turned from the stove to hand me a tomato as red and perfect as a gift.

The sun has crested the roof of the pharmacy across the square, bathing the room in shadow. A few cars remain in the parking lot, but I have waited long enough. Abandoning caution, I go to the customer counters and extract from them three built-in ashtrays. However, they yield nothing, nothing but butts. Not even a voided check or a torn withdrawal ticket. The only vaguely promising thing is a wad of tissue stained with a frosty pink lipstick on which a series of numbers has been totaled, the sum underscored twice in a hand so fierce that the paper has torn. But it is less than $600.

I upend a trash can with my foot, scattering more butts, and, this time, some paper. But there are only three of the mint-green deposit stubs that I am looking for, and two are blank. The other has been carefully scratched out so that prying eyes such as mine cannot make out the total.

My activity seems to have stirred Collins. I can hear a faint rustling coming from beyond the door. Something about the sound, the complexity of it maybe, the hiss of a shoe sliding across the marble floor, makes me realize that it is unlikely that his error is simply a matter of a single deposit. The three thousand was certainly an accumulation of botched transactions. Who knows? Maybe in an hour-long revery of nose picking, he took in ten thousand, handed out seven, and never knew the difference.

Concealed by shadows, unseen, I take the tellers' counter in a single leap, flashing me back to the days I spent jumping fences as a kid, chasing Irish kids through back yards, tossing fragments of brick after them once they were sure not to turn and fight. Never mind that I am half-Irish. The Irish genes recessed, the Italian took over, tinting my skin, overwhelming my face with a broken-looking nose. I carried the Bronx to Connecticut on my face.

Connecticut!

Land of soaring real-estate values!

The house is the only investment I have ever made that has appreciated. Median value in this village and the surrounding area is above two hundred. Eighteen years from now, the house will be mine, if I can make the mortgage payments, if I can cover the fiddling I did last month to keep a nonpayment from showing up on the books. I got a good price on the house. The developer went belly up and I put in a bid for the place at auction.

For my money, I got 1,500 square feet, a bit less than an acre of land, and a view, beyond the yard, of a tangle of witch hazel and maple saplings. I've learned something of wildlife since leaving the city. This is a rich land.

I am mildly concerned about Collins. Perhaps I am wrong about the vault. Perhaps it absorbs heat, turns into an unvented oven. Perhaps it really doesn't allow any air.

I approach the door. I don't want to let him out; neither can I leave him in. It occurs to me that, at some point, I must release him. The vault is always open during business hours.

I rest my cheek against the burnished steel door. It is warm, not what I had expected.

"Mr. Arango? Are you standing out there?"

His voice is either weakened by exhaustion and inadequate oxygen or undone by steel.

"How are you in there, Brian?"

"How am I?" He seems surprised by the question.

"Well?"

"I'm all right."

"How are you feeling? Are you lying down?"

"No."

If I release him, is there the possibility of violence? Would he come after me? Could it be that I have driven him to that?

"Are you hot? Is it very hot in there?"

"Pretty hot."

"Why don't you lie down for a while?" I suggest.

"On the floor?"

"It's clean enough." I listen for the telltale grunt to be sure he has followed instructions. "Are you lying down?"

Hesitantly, he says that he is.

"All right. I want you to look in your wallet. I want you to check your pockets to see if there's anything in there that would tell us what might have happened."

"I can't."

"Why not?"

"I already put that stuff on your desk. Remember?"

I do. That was before the air conditioning shut off. "Stay here," I say.

Of course, I find nothing of note in the small pile of possessions on my desk. Not even the pocket notebook, page after page filled with his inky pothooks, shows anything helpful. Fingering his wallet, I am certain that I will be depressed by whatever I find in it. The photograph on his driver's license will have been taken on the day he crushed his glasses and repaired them with wire and masking tape; I will find his fat, flattened image peering through milky lamination at nothing more valuable than last year's train schedule, receipts from the grocery store, the warranty on his Timex, a chit from the dry cleaner's, an old lottery ticket. And—what? A few dollars. Certainly not the three thousand I seek. So depressed am I by my imagined summation of Collins's life that I cannot bring myself to examine the contents of his wallet.

The phone rings.

I wonder what standards law schools use when admitting and rejecting applicants. Are there special dispensations for mothers and housewives long out of—or never in—the work force? Have endowments been established to encourage women professionals? Are there generous scholarships?

Jennie! Tennis is out, torts are in! But the children are still young. Peter only began school this year, and Melissa is just three.

Jennie's days have been considerably fuller since I gave the part-time housekeeper the sack and canceled the service of the lawn man. The latter I claimed to have caught smoking pot in the garage when he was supposed to have been laying in wood chips by the patio; the former I fired on the pretext of suspicion. I told Jenny I did not trust the housekeeper alone in the house, which gave rise, as I knew it would, to accusations of racism. We could afford neither sweeping nor weeding, but I hid this from Jennie. I softened the blow to the maid as best I could by giving her severance of sorts: I took her to the attic and presented her with four silver candlesticks, a present to Jennie from her first wedding. The housekeeper muttered confused, Spanish-accented thanks as we creaked down the hanging wooden stairs from the attic.

I care nothing for a clean house, and as for the gardening, Jennie doesn't mind it, so long as I take on the heaviest jobs, trucking soil from one corner to another, hauling the moaning old power mower over the lawn each Saturday. Gardening comes naturally to her. She understands plants, feels out their moist roots in the soil, frees the tendrils from the grasp of hardy weeds. She can tug an unwelcome invader from the earth whole. Unlike me, Jennie grew up in the suburbs.

She laughs at my ignorance, points out the strangling power of a morning glory, pulls up rocks like scabs, and is unruffled by the sight of the raw exposed earth beneath, the churning of earthworms and sow bugs. She laughs when I tour the perimeter of the yard, a pencil in one hand and an Audubon guide in the other, cataloging my holdings in nature.

"Mark? Are you still there? Baby, it's nearly eight."
"Jennie?"
"Who else would you expect to call you at this hour?"
I speak her name again, but it chokes itself out.
"Are you okay?"
I nod. "Yuh. You?"
"I'm fine. It's nearly eight, though."
Words crowd up too quickly for me to speak them. What has brought me to this? Is it the three thousand dollars? The collection letters from the credit companies? Or the dunning notes, stamped *Third Notice* in muddy red ink, from Jennie's rat-faced gynecologist? Or is it that I myself have arranged a liaison with a woman down the street? Jennie is to take the children to New York on Saturday for an afternoon of shopping and a Broadway matinee. I am to betray my wife while she is away. I cannot control desire.

"Mark? Should I come over there?"
"It's all right."
"I've never heard you sound so strange."
"I know."
"Mark?"
"There's an irregularity here," I say.
"I'm coming over. I'll be right there."
I have fifteen minutes.

. . .

Join the corps, Jennie! Think of the successes you would surely enjoy rigging mergers, blocking acquisitions, readying stock offerings! Imagine the comfort you could give families by preparing their wills and testaments! The power you would wield nailing down real-estate deals! Think, just think, of the money—the money that you yourself made—in your own hands!

I total up Collins's drawer in minutes. As a management trainee, long ago, I spent six months on the floor of a branch office, and I can flash bills through my hands so quickly that the images blur together.

I come up $250 over, and I am confused for a moment, until I realize that I have counted in a dummy packet of fives, the one that is loaded with explosives and orange dye, set to go off if it passes the magnetic sensors in the front door. That taken into account, I arrive at the same place Collins did several hours ago, $3,130 long.

I take a breath and begin the process of reduction. A ten from here, two twenties, a fifty, another twenty, a fistful of tens, a pack of twenties. Out of the drawer, these bills grow in stature: to a banker, a bill in a cash drawer is meaningless, an expression of currency in its purest form, a three-dimensional representation of service and product. But in my hands, it becomes, again, *money.*

I write up a new tally sheet for Collins, taking care to initial it at the top, as I do every afternoon. I staple the withdrawal slips and clip together the checks by clearance zone. The separated bills lie expectantly on the cleared counter.

The pile is too large to fit in my wallet, too conspicuous to be stored in my pants pocket. I split the pile in two and stow the halves in the breast pockets of my jacket, where they nestle comfortably in the silky lining.

I slide Collins's drawer from the desk and carry it back to the vault. "I'm coming in!" I announce, and tug at the door.

It is warm inside. Collins has removed his glasses, his jacket, and his tie, and has sprawled on the floor, his head canted against the far wall. At first glance, he seems lifeless, as if he had been thrown back and killed in an explosion, but his head jerks as I enter the chamber.

"You're totaled," I say, and slip the drawer into its slot in the wall.

"You found it? Where was it?"

"It wasn't any single thing," I say, trying to keep my cool, but my voice betrays me, leaps half an octave, like a flag being hoisted to signal the lie. "It was just a series of bookkeeping mistakes—debits to credits, vice versa, a miscount . . ."

For a moment he regards me, but I can't make out any suspicion in his dull eyes. He sits up. "I can go now?"

I feign surprise. "Of course."

I offer him a hand up, which he accepts. He is not as heavy as I had expected. Standing unsteadily, he claws his glasses from his shirt pocket, pushes them on his face.

"Okay," I say. "Let's go."

Outside, the air is slippery and warm. The sun is fully set, and the first stars are out. The half-moon is high, glowing weakly. The sky still holds a faint, bluish cast. A truck spins by on Route 41, and I can feel the faint rumbling of its passing in the concrete.

Collins trudges to his car. "Good night!" I call out to him. "Drive safely."

He looks at me, fumbles with his car keys.

"See you tomorrow!" I say. He drops his keys. "Nine o'clock!"

"Nine o'clock," he repeats. He wrenches the car door open, climbs in, and revs the motor twice before pulling out.

Now I am irrevocably tied to him; the bond is as sure as a shackle and chain. This web is always expanding. Secrets are unbreakable.

I am alone in the dark. My pockets bulge with money.

Behind me, my bank squats in the humid air, its round plastic logo glowing green like a cat's eye over the front door. Beggar-men, extend your tin cups tonight, for I have money in my hands again! I know it doesn't go far, and soon it will be gone.

But sooner, sooner, Jennie will arrive. She will roll down the window and consider me, her husband.

And I will follow my wife home. **Q**

Licensed for Private Exhibition Only

Now me—no matter what it is I do, to me he says, "Oh, what are you doing that for?" No matter what! Could be ice chips, how full I fill the cups, or the cuticle on his finger I pick at too long or too hard. Also, maybe something I drag over from home for him is not now in a pleasing shade.

Her, he picks up the phone on his bedside and says, "Hey, let me have your Boston cream pie slice. If you don't want it."

I say, "What are you doing that for?" and jerk on his fingers, and he says, "Tina, what are you doing that for?" about me, and into the phone he says, "Coppertone, we are coming over *en entourage*!"—him from his cranked-up bed, the sheet dipping between his bent-up knees.

He is pushing back the tray table, and is fighting off the sheet, and has got one leg dangling over the side of the bed already, and hangs up the phone wrong, and I am seeing his ankle, and it is starting me to thinking this crazy thing about how his ankle is in the factual window daylight; it is like nothing that suits him, with a black hair here and there, sprouting here and there, like something struggling to grow up in a rock crack and not doing too well, and I am thinking of how he looks to be riding his motorcycle, his hair styled wind-slicked-back, every hair scraped back by force and then going crazy out the back like flames licking air and sunlight, like joy even. I start to wondering things, and then think the thing that is important: that he does not call me Tina, he calls me Moonface is my name, and now with her Coppertone, I am Tina again.

"Grab that bottle of wine there, Tina, okay?" he says.

Boredom is what I tell myself I feel. We are there, him knocking on the door frame in a little rhythm, leaning forward some in the chair from eagerness, and from must be pain, too, me behind using my weight, pushing and trying to steer him around the sharp turn into her corner room, jerking the chair an inch or two to get him lined up so we go in straight and don't bang and scrape metal on wood.

This lady in there clicks off the TV and pulls the little chain on her reading light, and looks up at the two of us. She is a blond person with short curly hair, big shoulders and jaw.

"Hi, Troy. Is this her?" she says, and she smiles, using muscles in her face I never thought to even think about.

I say, "Hey," to this woman, and my hand waves itself at her, nothing planned.

Her bed is a messy place, a long-time home for a person, like the dogs' beds get sometimes when every night they just sleep there night after night, year after year, and things are ground in. Her bed is not that bad, but my mind does do an easy goose step to the dogs' beds, because her sheets are rumpled and there is a coffee spill and it does not look like this morning's coffee either. Her own flowered pillowcase from home must be on one of her pillows, a pillowcase with turquoise and red flowers, Hawaiian-looking, orchidy things; full-blown, noisy flowers with wide-open mouths, the whole thing soon surely ready for a run-through on the Maytag, but the right person has not noticed this, and it will not be me to notice it for them. Also, there are catalogues lying around on the covers, so I guess she has been ordering things for herself, or doing her Christmas shopping early, I am to suppose. And on her table tray is a slice of the pie he wants, and alongside it there is a clean fork.

He is buggy, trying to get me to get his chair in some right place he has in his mind, without taking his eyes off the woman in the bed, and I finally get him where he wants to be, and he rests his foot up on the metal bed frame, like it is what he always does, you know, like sidling up to someplace, maybe a bar, and fine, so I settle in the vinyl armchair off to the side and pull my legs up under me and cross my arms hard and listen to things myself in my own head that will help me, and I calm down like this.

"I am going on a safari to Kenya," Coppertone says, "when I get out of here."

Neither of us, Troy or me, says one thing to that, so after a while she shrugs and calls down to the nurse on the speaker intercom asking for fresh ice, ice chips for the plastic pitcher setting on her tray table, and Troy picks up the wine bottle and goes to work on it with a corkscrew he carried in here on himself. Maybe in his robe pocket. I think about getting up and that I could be lining up three Styrofoam cups on the metal chest of drawers, and decide that I will when I want to be doing something. He is still fixing the wine bottle anyway. The ice comes, and so I get up, and grind some cups upside down, which works good enough to fill them, and they will be kind of wine slushes, I am thinking, so I tear the top off the paper on a bendy straw, and accordion it down, and blow the accordion paper toward the cool, pine-smelling, chromy bathroom, where something of hers pink and nylon is hung up on a hanger on the shower rod. I cannot see it too well, so I am only guessing at what it is, but I am a woman who rinses out things and my guesses are good. The bendy straws are what the nurse gave me from the pocket of her skirt when I asked her for some straws. The nurse is black, and her I do like a great deal, which is how I usually feel toward people, but some are exceptions, I am coming to know.

Lace smoke snippets, it looks to be, slipping out the side of her mouth, Coppertone's goddamned whip cracking out a match lighting up a filter cigarette. And next, she is polite and passing around the box of truffles her grandmother sent her; they are big, the size of golf balls rolled first in cocoa powder and then in white powdered sugar, and they are special things. They make the wine taste sour, though, like the kids harp on me saying orange juice tastes to them after they have eaten their pancakes and syrup first, exactly in the wrong order. But the wine is cold and nice, like a wine slush is supposed to be.

She is looking over at me sitting in the corner, in the vinyl armchair where I am. My face feels good on my head, it just does is all. She sits there in her bed, staring up over her cup, her lips, her mouth still on the cup, like she is drinking; her eyes she is lifting, and looks at me, and I know this is something different for her, the way we are, Troy and I, or maybe just the way I am. The way we are is a couple, and she has only seen him as him, and the way I am is moon-faced, with my black hair, and that is something alongside his blond straight hair, and chiseled upper lip, and kind of pouting bottom lip, and smartness, and we are a couple with children at home. My whole self says, "Yes, honey," at her without saying a word, and she hears me, I know she does, and so she turns away from me to where Troy is, anywhere where I am not.

She and Troy talk hospital talk, patient talk, about is there any sense to anything anyway, and tell each other how hard things are and how much they are in pain and what a time they have.

Troy says, "I am going to get really well. I am going to get more well than Tina over there. I might work in this hospital."

Coppertone nods. "I will never come back to this hospital, or any other, when I get out," she says.

I watch them through slits in my eyes, and they prism as if I am seeing them out of a fly's eyes.

"I know how old people feel now, so that is good," Coppertone says to somewhere, off at the wall, it looks like.

"That's right, we sure know that," Troy says.

Well, it could have waited, there's time, I think. It is nothing I am in a hurry to know, how old people feel, though what I say is, "That is right, you do, and I don't," which is what they want to hear.

Troy says, "This pie is good. Here, Tina, have a taste," and turns around and looks at me hard, because he knows how I feel on matters.

I hold up my hand with the truffle, which means no, and slit my eyes at them again, all around the room slitted, into the bathroom, all around the room into places they do not even know about in this room.

"I think I was put in here for a reason," Troy says to Coppertone, forgetting about me, and getting to what he always gets to. I can hear it coming, that God did it to him for a reason, that God selected him out and flung him around His head like he was a rock on the end of a rope because he was not living the best life. God was on to him.

I say, "Well, you are going to be out of here faster than you can say Jack Rabbit," is what I say, and push my skirt up to look at my knees.

Neither of them says anything, but there is something in the air, and Coppertone passes Troy the last cigarette from her soft pack as she smiles a small smile and says to me, "Honey? Call down to the nurses' station and tell them it is time for my medication, would you be such a darling?"

I heave myself out of the armchair, untangling my arms and legs, setting the rest of the truffle I ate only part of on her bedside table. "I will just walk," I say, hanging myself with my arm like a gate hinge on the back of Troy's chair, then swinging around his neck to give him a kiss.

The nurse follows me in, carrying tiny paper pill cups and two evil hypodermics on a tray, and there they are, Troy and Coppertone, smoking up the room, and her now, both hands in the bedside table drawer pawing through VHS cassettes, cigarette sticking straight out her mouth, eyes squinted up, like mine are when I am doing fly eyes. Troy is laughing, and looks to be in a slingshot, slung back low like he is in his wheelchair, blowing smoke rings high in the room, roping dead patient spirits and reading cassette warnings out loud off videocassettes. But he is doing one smart thing; his legs he has up on her bed now to move the blood in a different direction, so it does not pool in his ankles and make clots and kill him and end this whole thing.

I stare around the room with eyes that feel bigger and bigger, as swoosh, the nurse opens the window wide, which slides up like on air, sucking the smoke out of the room like the thing above my stove at home, some machine somewhere out there in the night just turned on, and I stand back a minute to watch, and it is something, it is working, and I am thinking about the smoke sucked out of that room, like one huge spirit now with smoke ropes fraying fast around its neck, now here with us, now choking us and causing sickness, then just gone. Just not here. I stare with big eyes at the easiness of it, then catch myself as the nurse bumps me while moving around the foot of the bed, and so I grab for the ashtrays, to be dumping them out, and tidying up, rinsing them with cold bathroom water, smiling new and wide at the nurse as she nurses Troy and Coppertone, since their medication schedules are the same. I splash some wine in our chewed-up, tooth-marked cups, where it has been drunk low, offer around what truffles are left, and in the bathroom, I put on some pearl lipstick I find lying out there on the basin, and comb my hair up in a tight twist with tap water, and stick in a few bobby pins I dig out of my tote. My wet hands I roll in the hem of her nightgown hanging up there on the shower rod, until they are as dry as nylon can get anything that is wet, all the time thinking that the room is cleaned up now and nothing is the same and things will get better. When I come out of the bathroom, I feel new and good and clean, and say, "Come on, you all! Let's get well in here!" and I clap my hands a couple of times.

Where they had their shots, they rub themselves with hands made tight into fists, and look at me, electrified and standing in the bathroom high-watt light, and I am a thing to make them blink huge, slow blinks that take time. Then one of them says, "Come on. I guess we should brush our teeth or something."

"My teeth are fine," the other one says, and that is the end of that, as I know they are slipping back down into their sickness, where they want to be, no matter what so.

Fine.

Fixing my lipstick with my finger, I get behind Troy and lean forward and say to be trying, because I am his wife, "Let us go on back to your room now, honey, okay? That shot is going to be working and you can sleep. You don't want to be staying up all night looking at some dumb movie." Troy does not say anything to me, so I go over to the woman's bed and start looking through her catalogues and asking her about the things in them she likes. Her shot is working and she is nicer.

Coppertone says, "Look here, Tina. Look at this night-gown and robe I ordered. Just put it on my Visa card."

I look.

"Now, what have you done with your hair, Tina?" Troy says, leaning sideways and back in his chair, holding his cigarette out away from him, uphanded.

"I just pushed it up and stuck some pins in it. Nothing."

"Oh," he says, and is gone, I know, because I am watching for it. I get back in my armchair, toes hooking over his wheel spokes, and we get into more wine, and they start talking and banging VHS cassettes until they decide to screen one even though it is late, a weird movie set in Texas Troy shows over and over at home. I only hate it more every time I see it is all I can say about this movie. I curl in on myself, my knees tight up against my chest, my back curving like something fitted snug in a shell just opened enough to see out of, and it is like this that I nod through the credits, then sleep like a baby halfway through the movie, until I wake with Troy shaking my shoulder: "Help me, Tina. I got to lie flat, help me get in there with Coppertone until the movie is over."

We clear off the catalogues, and put the movie on pause, and Coppertone moves over to the side closest to the radiator, and I help Troy and straighten out his legs, and get his back fixed up flat, and find a pillow and stuff it up under his knees. I even get extra pillows from his room next door and put them where he says he wants them—it is an ordeal—and I fix Coppertone up with some cream she wants for her hands and the lip gloss for her lips, which are cracking, and I settle them in like babies—but easier than the boys at home, who always kick and never need a thing like sleep and quiet, and who wake each other up if one of them ever does make it to sleep. These two are easy to settle. I go in Coppertone's bathroom and run a washcloth over my face, then climb back in the vinyl armchair, the movie flickering in the pitch-black room, Coppertone and Troy in her little hospital bed cranked up just a little for both of them, Coppertone and him in her bed making two red cigarette eyes like a crazy thing that kind of scares me if I look at it too long, smoke breath making quick for the window, no sound from the movie, as it is too late in the night for sounds that are not screams or snores or moans or something crackling in on the intercom.

Coming close to sleep, my mind moves around thoughts better left alone, like smoke circles and ropes, wispy things, things better left alone, I guess.

So I think about how we got into this place, what happened, which is wonder enough and easy. Easy as being worn out, which is what he was. He was tired is all. Nothing happened. It was just his way of taking his leave on things that have gotten hard, his way of saying he needs a rest, or maybe needs a change is what it is. It is his surprisedness at the hardness that I do not understand, as I am not surprised by much and everything seems hard anyway. He is the one who brings up God, about being at the end of God's rope is the way it seemed for him, God twirling him around His head is how he came to be skidding in that beautiful arc, a slid arc, a gorgeous arc that went on and on across black almost-liquid-boiled-up asphalt, goldenrod and ragweed bunching up on each side of the road, smearing the only colors there were that he saw and remembered. God's colors. Golds like the sun.

So far, thank God, God does not have me at the end of some rope knocking my brains out and breaking all my bones and cooking me up in boiling asphalt. He is giving me a chance here to be quiet is how I see it.

I am happy. There are truffles to bite into, to see what is in the middle, and apple juice if I want to go down the hall for it. I can sip my wine as slow as I want, pull pins out of my hair, drop them each one on the floor, and shake my hair loose, maybe dance a little, rubbing my arm, dance alone in the dark to the movie music if I care to use the earphones. I can call the kids and see what they are up to, then climb back in the vinyl armchair, put my head down, and be sleeping curled up, my hair waterfalling over like rapids over my crossed arm, and wait like that. Wait maybe for God's hand on my hair, which is the way He might come to me. I can sleep anywhere waiting for that. I just let it be hard while it is hard, without going crazy for it to get easy. **Q**

From the District File

Mr. M.—I say Mr. M. to exercise caution—is a rich man by my standards. I respect him, because although he has ample resources, he has never left the neighborhood. He treats everyone as an equal. He is generous with children who collect for their clubs. There is nothing ostentatious in his apartment. Of course, it is large. One never gets the sense that food or drink is lacking, but one is served modest portions. There is no condescension. One is greeted warmly and one is sped on one's way warmly. But one feels—one *knows*—that behind it all there is an amplitude of resources, a solid wealth that informs his every move with strength and confidence. So you can imagine my astonishment when one day, at a mid-distance of several blocks, I saw a police officer strike him on his head with a truncheon. I was standing idly by the curb, enjoying the early spring sun, taking in the scene at large, of which he was merely a small point. I remember thinking he must be instilling more pride in the officer by favoring him with a kind word or two. It was a common maneuver of his with the many public servants in our immediate area, and it had the effect of making the sun all the more warming. And then, without my really registering it, Mr. M. suddenly raised his hands and his voice, and the officer gave him a distinct crack on the head. It was like a little bit of thunder in a clear sky. I was shocked, of course, and began rushing to him, until I saw that he was himself scurrying in my direction, his hand, leaking blood, pressed to his scalp. He was white with rage. "My dear Mr. M.," I said, "what has happened? How can I help you?" He pushed by, taking no notice of me. Ahah, I thought, just a bit irritated, now the fur will fly. And I sauntered, casually, near the offending police officer, to have a good view of the action. He was a brutish but happy-looking man with thick lips, heavy limbs, and weak blue eyes. His face reflected no anxiety over his action, nor did he seek to move. You're in for it now, my man, I thought. Mr. M. is no mere nobody. The minutes extended to the quarter hours, and finally an entire hour had passed. No siren, no Mr. M., no squadron chief, no public official, no supporters, no onlookers (except myself). Everything was as usual. What, then, had Mr. M. done? Was it possible that he had transgressed the law? Was there more to it than met the eye? I went home to think about it.

The next day I observed Mr. M. in the postal substation. He had better color, wore a bandage on his head, and took no notice of anybody. He was armed with a bundle of official-looking letters, and I covertly watched him feverishly licking stamps. He was in a great sweat. How clever of him, I thought. That was the way to do it. One never got anywhere except through the proper channels, the proper officials. And Mr. M. knew them all, no matter how tucked away. A few letters in the proper quarters and our policeman would be in knots for years, perhaps even in disgrace. How devilishly patient and clever of Mr. M. I wanted to accost him and congratulate him on the correctness of his action, but I could tell he was in no mood to be interrupted. Even one of his little charges, a pretty girl in a brown uniform, was put off with a brusque "Later. Later. Can't you see I'm busy?" In fact, the girl had wanted only to say hello to a favorite contributor and customer. Mr. M. rushed out, looked carefully in both directions, and sped away. He was not done yet, I could see, not by a long shot. Nor was I.

Nearly a week later, I was walking by Mr. M.'s building. I knew his quarters and looked up. All the shades were drawn. This I understood. It was clearly war, and these were siege conditions. Mr. M.'s tactics were equal to his strategy. Letters take time. Officials and their subofficials are slow to move. Bureaucracy is like a sleeping monster. But once awakened, it must be fed. And Mr. M.'s letters would awaken it. As I pondered it all, a drama took shape before my eyes. From one end of the street came Mr. M., unshaven and a bit seedy. From the other end, strolling smugly, came the very same officer who had cracked his head. They saw each other simultaneously. People smiled and cleared out of the way. I could see Mr. M.'s thoughts. Could he reach the entrance of his building before the police officer? They both increased their pace, but Mr. M., key at the ready and nearly running, seemed to have the advantage. And then the police officer stamped his feet quickly in place as if he, too, were running, and at the same time rapped his truncheon vigorously on a nearby vehicle, actually denting it, I think. Mr. M. turned tail and ran, disappearing around the nearest corner. The police officer roared with good humor and continued his stroll. As he walked by me, I pretended not to notice him. I looked at the sky, as if there were large birds migrating. I felt a sharp jab in my lower back. His truncheon. I looked, he winked and walked on. Smile, you beast, I thought, rubbing my back, your days are numbered.

Two days later, I was out early, after a restless night. I thought greeting the sun might lift my spirits, along with coffee and a crumpet in my favorite café. An old car was parked in front of Mr. M.'s building. I did not recognize the driver. Soon Mr. M. came out with his wife, a nondescript, stoutish woman, two tired-looking, puny children, and a miscellany of bundles. He pushed them all roughly into the car, handed the driver a fistful of money, and spoke angrily to his wife, who cried throughout. "Go, go," he said, waving the car on, even as his wife reached out her hand. Unsuccessfully. I understood at once. No hostages to fortune. The man did not compromise. He had no illusions. He waited until the car was far down the street, then turned to go in. "Wait. Wait," I cried. He turned in some fear, then, seeing me, paused. His eyes were bloodshot, his hair seemed suddenly streaked with white. I grasped his hand tightly in mine. "I admire you enormously,"

I said. "And you will win. You will win!" He looked at me a moment, then burst into tears, turned and slammed the door in my face. I never saw him again.

What happened after is, typically, not clear. I was alert for days for whatever drama was to come. But no visible, concluding event occurred. The shades remained drawn, the police officer continued to patrol, even looking up at Mr. M.'s windows. Once, I thought I saw Mr. M. peeking out, but could not be sure. I followed the mailman into the vestibule one morning and saw that Mr. M.'s mailbox was stuffed with mail. Had he perhaps joined his wife and children to fight from another front? But if so, why? The rumors started after a middle-of-the-night visit by police officers in plain clothes. The witnesses were few and contradictory. They had broken the door in and come out with some materials. But what materials? The door was resealed until an auctioneer came and removed everything, selling it and sending the check, it was said, to his wife. An old man on the top floor said Mr. M. had hung himself from a heating pipe and it was the smell that had brought the police. He insisted he knew the smell of dead bodies. No one believed him. My own view was that Mr. M. had discovered that his allies and contacts in the bureaucracy had been swayed by new ideologies and loyalties, and he had wisely and swiftly removed himself, his family, and his wealth elsewhere. But even his wealth was questioned. Someone who attended the auction of his goods said they had brought little, that the furniture was shabby, the linens worn, the clothes patched. And the money went not to his wife but to the state, for taxes and fines. It is true that visible signs of Mr. M.'s wealth were few, had always been few, but I trusted my feelings about him. There is no question he is gone, at least for the immediate future. His apartment has been subdivided, and the new tenants live like the rest of us. The little girls and boys do not do so well there, but one or two of them, already growing older and wiser, remember that once, whenever they knocked at that particular door, whatever they were selling was bought at once, and doubly or trebly, with a smile. It is for them a memory of another time, an inkling of what history must be. Someday the dreams they are now having of the old man who knows the smell of dead bodies will be history, too. And the children will be still older and wiser. But for the moment, they do not ask him for anything. His door remains closed.

All they know is that he is behind the door.

That his nose is twitching like a dog's. **Q**

Jerry

"If animals could catch us," Hanker says, "they'd eat us. The only reason anyone ever eats a vegetable is that's all they can catch."

Hanker is big, a cannonball horse. Me, I'm a shrimp. We've been up all Sunday reroofing my uncle's barn, which my uncle politely calls a garage. Big cheap favor for him, but it's acres of work and my hands feel like they're still falling off. About an hour ago we were starting to bake around the edges, so now we're down in the El Toledo, a hole of a bar that Hanker, if he ever owned a bar, would wish was his. On the way over, his Corvette hit a spaniel, one of those dogs that looks like it ought to be carrying slippers everywhere. Just stunned him, but still, Hanker wouldn't stop.

"So." He's chewing. Hanker's my brother-in-law and he's eating an extremely rare hamburger, so rare I can barely watch. There's a turquoise bandanna that just fits knotted around his forehead. "Did I tell you?"

I shake my head. That starts it. We have these rules every time we eat here: Whoever runs dry on stories buys. I don't know why.

"Your sister," Hanker says, "brought home this lion. She tells me she's going out to buy a kitten, but she comes back with this thing that thinks it's a lion."

"What'd you do?"

"Do? It's running everything. Won't meow, just looks at you like you're dinner. Eats plants and gives me the willies. We've got a real nice hateful relationship. The thing spends all day waiting for me to feed the tropical fish. I know it wants those fish." Hanker is swabbing his burger in the ketchup lake at the side of his plate.

"Huh," I say, trying not to sound too interested too early.

"At work last week, we had a tiny gray kitten climb up the fourth-floor fire escape and then in our office window. Kept him all day. Had him dancing on the Xerox machine."

"You can't Xerox a kitten." Hanker rolls a single and stuffs it in the top of his empty Rolling Rock bottle like a flag. "What'd you do? Push its face into the glass?"

"Nope. He was just standing on top, so we'd hit the button and *he'd* put his nose right into it. We had copies all over the walls. Four paws and whiskers."

Hanker shrugs. "Real cute," he says. "You were lucky."

I'm trying to ignore the car commercials on the tube, since I need a new one, so I stare at the model Budweiser wagon up over the bar. It's about two feet long, with twelve tiny horses pulling it. "Ever think of just giving up, going to Montana and riding a horse somewhere?" I ask.

"What? You want a horse?" Hanker says. "My boss has this horse he can't get his kids off of with a crowbar. There's another one. I ride it just once, as a favor, to show those kids how, and the thing takes off into all these fence posts, trying to rub me out."

I'm smiling. "You don't have much of a paranoia problem." On TV they're fishing for steelheads.

Hanker goes on with his burger. "Ha," he says, "take my kids. For a while they had gerbils, then one of them went crazy and tried to burrow its way out of the aquarium. The other one they took on a trip and put black paper around the cage so it wouldn't get carsick? We get there—it's baked."

"Cooked?"

Hanker nods and pushes leftover hamburger parts around his plate. "Hey," he says quietly, "now how about your tropical fish? Some of those are sardine-sized. You could pan-fry up a mess of neon tetras, but they'd probably fade. It'd serve them right. All they do is go back and forth."

I'm almost ready to change the subject, but I've started coming up with dog stories in spite of myself.

"We are a pretty screwed-up bunch," Hanker says. "I

mean pet them and eat them. I bet if pets tasted better, there'd be a lot fewer in this world. How about those little birds?" Hanker has this happy look, like he's thinking of a long-lost banquet. "Maybe batter-dipped? Probably crunchy."

Hanker's staring at himself in the mirror. He taps the bottle on the bar. "Take my first wife's dog," he says. "Barked at everything, including me, for years. We move up to the lake and all of a sudden I find out he's a rock dog. Goes swimming for them. Even in winter. I mean big things, actual two-pounders. At night he left them all cold and slippery on the stairs. He knew what he was doing. I'd come down in the dark and, bang, lose another toe. Ron's there listening in the kitchen and thumping his tail."

I try not to look impressed.

"Same dog," Hanker says, "almost gets me arrested. We're at a convenience store, late, lots of drunk college kids around, and Ron runs in, chomps through the cellophane into a box of doughnuts on the bottom shelf, carries them to the door, sets them down, clamps his paw on top, and looks around until some kid lets him out. The kid says, 'Hey, mister, you know your dog just stole a box of doughnuts?' Of course I knew. He ate half of them before I could drag him to the car."

"Doughnuts are bad for dogs," I say.

"Pets turn on you," Hanker tells me, like it's the word of God. "Don't trust nature."

I shake my head. "Not true."

"Yeah? Take insects. An insect's main problem is it has way too much body surface for its volume and is always losing body fluids. When they land on you, they're searching for a drink. They'll even drink your tears. Spiders drank my tears." He gives me a quick shudder.

I look in my beer. "Must be spider heaven."

"You can tell a lot about a house by its pets." Hanker folds his arms, stretching his gray T-shirt sleeves. "Get a bad one, one everybody hates, and things are shot to hell. You get bad pets around bad people."

I'm watching to see if Hanker hears the implications of what he's said. Then he starts his slow proud smile. "Been awhile since I didn't know where I stood."

"I've had only good pets," I say.

"Ha. Run out of cans of whatever and your dog'll be looking at you like you could use some tenderizer."

We watch golf for a while, then horse jumping. When it's later than we both realize, Hanker pays for everything. "Next time," he says.

When Hanker drops me off, it's dark, and the funny thing is, my dog isn't out in the run where I left him with his food. When my foot touches the back deck, his paws scratch into the sliding door's glass. A white note is taped on the outside from my landlord neighbors, saying he was making a racket so they brought him in.

My hall light has been broken for a while, so I take the flashlight out of the extra mailbox for the empty basement apartment. I turn it on, shoot it around inside through the curtains, and unlock.

There's white dust hanging in the beam and Jerry's staring at me, cold, yellow-eyed, but not snarling. The couch cushions are scattered. His paw covers the tear in the beanbag chair, while tiny white Styrofoam beads cling to his lips like foam. The rest are all over. They could be ant eggs.

Jerry barks low to the ground and I'm all set to shout, "Bad dog," but have the feeling I better not. **Q**

Blue Is the Color You Don't See Anymore

MICHELE *and* NAN *are sitting in a churchyard with blankets around them. It is night. In the background there is bright orange light from a fire.*

NAN: First they take a hatchet to the door. Even if the door is open. They do it anyway. Then they break things in your house. They break the mirrors and say it was the heat. This blender. They would have taken the hatchet to it if I had not grabbed it off the table and put it up under my robe.

MICHELE: Did you get the Marie Antoinette ring?

NAN: This is not the new kind made of plastic. This is the kind that only says off and on. There is no mix, whip, or liquefy to contend with. When you turn this thing on, it just does it. It does it all.

MICHELE: Because I did not get the Marie Antoinette ring.

NAN: They say with the cats, you take a pillowcase and throw them in there. But I have also heard that you do not worry about the cats. That they know where to go and can find air like we cannot.

MICHELE: All that I took was a book.

NAN: What book? Is it a good book?

MICHELE: A kid's book. *The Enchanted Island.* It was my favorite book. I can't believe all I brought was a book. Will they take the ring?

NAN: Think of their coats. Those big pockets. I have heard of cameras missing, hand-held calculators, designer telephones. What's the book about?

MICHELE: I don't remember. How can I tell her that I did not take the ring?

NAN: She will not think about the ring. She will ask how we are. She will ask how we survived. She will touch our faces as if she were blind and she was meeting us for the first time. She will curse herself for not having been here with us—to help.

Just think, it may last for days. It may be like those fires across the water, the ones that you can see if you stand on the piers. People walk down to see those fires. They walk down after dinner. Fathers bring their children and fathers point and tell their children how the wind might change, how—a little this way or a little that way—something else may burn.

MICHELE: I'm going in there. I'm going to get the ring.

NAN: See how far they let you get.

MICHELE: Oh, my God—I think I just heard the skylight go.

NAN: They did it. They will tell you it's the heat, but it's the hatchet. They throw the hatchet up into the air—Indian style—while the fire rages on. They play games of strength and skill.

MICHELE: How do you like these blankets?

NAN: I love these blankets.

MICHELE: These blankets could have been on dead people. These blankets could have burned flesh stuck to them.

NAN: These blankets are warm.

MICHELE: I'm going up to them when they leave. I'm going to ask if they can open wide their pockets so I can see in. What gives them the right? So big deal, they save our lives, throw our cats into pillowcases—they steal her Marie Antoinette ring, and they are not the men I waved to as a child on the street. It will be a thank-you for the blankets, but conversation.

NAN: Oh, I've had those before.

MICHELE: Yeah, but what if they don't put it out? What if everything goes?

NAN: You mean like the top to this blender? Because I just realized, I don't have the top to this blender. I will be right behind you when you look into their pockets. Fork up my blender top, I will say. Like me, they will be attracted by its sturdy construction. They will lift it and turn it as if it were a kaleidoscope. They will rest it on their coffee tables at home. Tell me something redeeming about the book. Tell me the book was made with horse glue and books are not made with horse glue any longer.

MICHELE: I do not know. There is a page in this book, in the front of this book, before the picture of the man in the book and the island he is on, and the page is made out of paper that you can see through. So if you get to this page, you can just barely see through to the man and his island on the next page, and it is as if the page is there before the picture to get you ready for how good the picture is; then without the paper over it, the picture is even better, and then what follows? You know what follows. The book follows, and it is better than the paper or the picture, because if you lose the book . . .

NAN: Let's say in a fire . . .

MICHELE: Right, in a fire, let's say—then you never forget the book if you've read it. And the book can be up there, in the fire, and it's all right. But the ring. A ring is not like a book. Made out of gold and a ruby in the middle and diamonds all around . . . When she gets here, tell her that we almost died.

NAN: Why?

MICHELE: Give me a match, I'll singe your hair.

NAN: What?

MICHELE: So she'll forget. So she'll be too worried about us to think about what's in there, or what's not in there.

NAN: You know she never wore the ring.

MICHELE: With the ruby and the diamonds and the gold, who would wear such a ring on a bus or a train?

NAN: The ring is to say this belonged to my mother and her mother before her. The ring is to say and before that it belonged to Marie Antoinette. The ring is to say maybe this was the ring Marie Antoinette wore when her head was chopped off. The ring is not to be worn.

MICHELE: What else do they do in our house?

NAN: They look through our pictures. They take the picture of Mom with the dog in her lap, she yawning and the dog yawning and Mom sitting on the steps of the porch with just a sheet around her, holding the dog. They take that picture and hold it up to the fire and nearly let it catch on fire before they pull it away. They tease us. They know we are sitting out here with their old blankets around our backs.

MICHELE: Blankets dead people have been wrapped in.

NAN: They let the fire burn and all the mirrors break. And it is not until the night is over and it is morning that they let the water from the hoses run.

MICHELE: By then she will have been here, touching our faces, smoothing back our singed hair, asking for the ring.

(Enter MIE, the grandmother, holding a chair, which she sets down on the grass. MICHELE and NAN go up to her and kiss her on both cheeks)

MIE: I once called a fork a fuck at your mother's wedding. Everyone was saying "dahling," it seemed to be the only thing to do—forget your rs. This was easy for a foreigner—to change the alphabet, I mean. Isn't that what all foreigners want to do, anyway? Change the alphabet? Make it like their own? Remove some letters? Besides this, have you thought about the plural s? What good is an s except to tell you there is more than one, and that you would already know, you would be able to see there is more than one. Two girls. There are two of you, each one of you is a girl. Why girls?

MICHELE: Why the chair?

MIE: Did you think I would join you on one of those blanket out here?

MICHELE: These blankets have dead people's skin clinging to them.

MIE: Where did she go, anyway?

MICHELE: She's run off with a fireman in his red truck, and they are going to make little fire babies forever and ever.

MIE: After the wedding, she yelled at me, and then I drove the car out onto the ice and waited there while they stood on shore and whispered loudly for me to come back to land, because they were afraid that the ice would break and that I would fall in while the ice-cold water came through the hole in the car, and then she came out to me, kind of sliding on the ice, the way you would have to do if you were not wearing skate but you were wearing shoe and you were trying to get across the ice, and then she put her face up to mine at the window and breathed on the window until I could not see her face any longer, and then she knocked on the door and I let her in, and she had a rim of snow at the bottom of her silver wedding dress from climbing about on the shore and waving at me while standing on tall rocks, and I remember I watched the snow melt around her dress to make a water stain that looked as if she had a ridge of mountain drawn at the bottom of her dress while she told me she was sorry, that really it was almost too easy to say fuck instead of fork and that she did not blame me and that she was sorry. It was after that that I gave her the ring off my finger, the Marie Antoinette ring with the ruby in the middle and the diamond all around.

MICHELE: Have you ever read *The Enchanted Island*?

MIE: No.

NAN: It is a wonderful book. The pages are glued together with horse glue, and they do not make books like that any longer.

MICHELE: Our cats are in pillowcases.

MIE: This is no place to wait for your house to burn down. Where is the bar? Where are the drink? Can we get into the Holy Water? Have they filled the basin with Sunday wine?

> TIM *is in a country home that is wrecked. He is holding a hammer in his hand. It is night. He is talking on the phone.*

TIM: Well, yes, it still runs; it's just a dent, a big black dent; the enamel flew off when I hit it. You're lucky I called. I could not have called, and then what would you have done the next weekend? You would have come up, you would have walked in the door, and you would have seen everything like this. No, I'm not going to clean it up, but it makes a difference you knowing. I think it still runs. *(He goes over to the washing machine and starts it)* See, listen, it still runs. *(He holds the phone in the washing machine)* Sure, it could be the faucet, but it isn't, just wait till it starts going, then you'll see. Fish. Fried fish. Mrs. Paul's. Yes, everyone knows there are no bones in Mrs. Paul's. God, wait till you see this place. No, I feel the same. Maybe tired. I'm a little more tired. I can't. Because your mattress is sticking half out the window. It wouldn't fit all the way and I couldn't bring myself to do it, anyway. I like the stripes. The stripes on the ticking. No, green, blue, and aqua. No, just green, blue, and aqua, no yellow. No yellow. I'm sure. I'd go check, but it's out the window. Right, only half out. Well, yeah, the halves are the same, but, Dad, I don't feel like going to the window. *(Washing machine starts going,* TIM *quickly puts the phone to it)* It's the washing machine. *(He begins to walk around the kitchen, putting everything into it, pots, plates, dishrags, salmon-mousse molds, a flint lighter made of metal for the oven range)* I'm doing a load. Just stuff. See, it works. (TIM, *still holding the hammer, thinks of putting it into the washing machine but does not)* God, it's so quiet here. I mean, what do you do for fun? Chase the bull? I'll bet you have . . . What? All right. *(He holds the phone away from his ear, tries to put the phone into the washer, but like the hammer he does not. He walks around the kitchen. Finally he yells into the phone)* Dad! Dad! DAAAD! Jesus Christ! I'm throwing a fit here and nobody seems to give a damn! Dad, I'm gonna do the oven next, the refrigerator. I can see your collection of beach glass! What? Yes. Really? Well, maybe it's just the girls throwing a fit, there may not be any fire. All right then, goodbye. *(He hangs up the phone, stands for a bit, then goes to the window and takes the jar of beach glass down. He goes to the washing machine and takes out each bit of beach glass one by one and dips it into the washing-machine water and then lifts each piece out to look at it wet under the light)*

> *Back in the churchyard with* MIE, MICHELE, *and* NAN, *but just as the lights come up,* ROGER *rides in on his bicycle.*

MIE: What's he doing here?

ROGER *(To the girls)*: Where's your mother?

MIE: She's off making red baby.

ROGER *(Going up to the girls)*: They give you these blankets? These are great blankets. These are like old army blankets. These last forever. They're as heavy as carpets. Keep these blankets. Don't give these blankets back.

MICHELE *(To* NAN*)*: Could this be a fair trade for a ring?

MIE: Tell him about the dead-people skin.

NAN: There's burned skin hanging off these blankets.

ROGER: That is added warmth.

MIE: Did you bring vodka?

ROGER *(Pulling things out of the bicycle basket)*: I have mini-franks, navel oranges, and tomatoes which you can eat like apples they are so good.

MIE: I hope if she comes she brings the vodka.

NAN: What if she never comes back? I mean, what if we left her in there or something?

MICHELE: What if she set the fire?

ROGER: What are you talking about? She's not in there. Why did you leave her in there? You didn't leave her in there.

MIE: She will be all right. I have heard they put you in pillow-case.

NAN: Left alone, maybe she has found air on her own and she's in some corner of the house that we never knew about.

ROGER: When did you see her last?

MIE: It was Christmas. I don't remember how I got home.

ROGER: Not you.

MICHELE: We went to bed. She said she was going out.

NAN: We watched her put her lipstick on, like we always do.

MICHELE *(To* MIE*)*: It was Tim—he put you in a cab. He said you kept on falling down. Your knees kept giving, he said.

NAN: As if knees could give flowers, chocolate, a second look, respect, a damn, a try, a darn . . .

MICHELE: It was Divine Providence that you made it into your house that night.

ROGER *(Looking at the burning house)*: If she was in there, they would have brought her out by now.

NAN: They need an audience, someone to watch them at their games of strength and skill.

MICHELE: That, or they are passing her back and forth, the ring on one's finger, the blender top in one's pocket, and she tumbling through midair, the flames from the fire just touching her hair.

ROGER: Well, someone should go in there and get her.

MIE: Yes, and bring out a bottle of vodka.

NAN: By now the bottle has exploded.

ROGER: I can't believe you left her in there.

NAN: Why are you here, Dad?

ROGER: I came by to watch.

NAN: You see, all he is missing is a child by his side, holding his hand, and he will watch the next thing go . . . And to think poor Tim is missing everything.

MICHELE: How is Tim? Has he set your country house on fire yet?

NAN: Had sex with the bull?

MIE: With those long finger, he always reminds me of my husband.

ROGER: He has put a hole into the washing machine with my hammer.

MICHELE: How do you know?

ROGER: He called to tell me.

MIE: Like my husband, Tim has always been very thoughtful.

NAN *(To* MICHELE*)*: I don't know why, after Tim was born cast in gold, they didn't realize much sooner how special he is.

MIE: He peed up into the amah's face and she didn't wash her face for day, the piss of a firstborn being very lucky.

NAN: She meant to say kiss, not piss.

MICHELE: Fork, not fuck.

ROGER: I'm going to get some wine.

MIE: Some vodka.

(ROGER *leaves. Nothing is said. A big sound of something falling is heard from the burning house.* MICHELE *looks at* NAN)

MIE: That is not her falling. That is some beam you have in your place.

NAN: Who knows if when you are dreaming that you are flying that you are not really flying?

MICHELE: Where do all the pigeons sleep?

MIE: Of course, I have not seen your mother in a while, so she might be heavier and she might sound like a beam if she fell.

NAN: Maybe I have flown to the piers and back and I don't even know it.

MICHELE: I believe they sleep down at the piers and feed on the floating condoms in the river.

NAN: Then why did you ask?

MICHELE: It is nice to have a theory backed up.

MIE: Where does it come from to say "taking" in a movie? Where does the movie go? Is there some hole in your body where it can fit? Does it go in the ear?

NAN: The delicatessen could go next, the way this wind is blowing, and it very well could be the delicatessen to go next.

MICHELE: And if the wind blows the other way?

MIE: The liquor store down the street.

NAN: It would be a grand explosion; for a change people in New Jersey would be watching us burn.

(ROGER *comes back with wine and vodka. The girls go up to him, checking his hair*)

MIE *(To the girls)*: What are you doing?

MICHELE: Checking for singed hair.

NAN: To see if the liquor store has caught yet.

ROGER: A toast.

MICHELE: For what?

ROGER *(Picking up book)*: I don't know. To this book. A toast to this book. It used to be my favorite book.

MIE: A toast, because now we have vodka and we are not in the fire.

NAN: Who knows, we might even be missing something. They say when you're drowning, it is the best feeling—your lungs explode—you see God—your lungs burn, maybe you see Him, too.

ROGER: I was in a fire once.

MIE: Are you saying *you* have seen God?

ROGER: I carried my dog down the fire escape under my arm; with the other hand, I held my jar of beach glass.

MICHELE: And what about the other stuff, the stuff that costs a lot of money, the stuff that's been in the family forever. The jewelry, the rings?

ROGER: I didn't think about that stuff. I thought about my beach glass, how I had saved it for so many years, how I liked looking at it on my shelf when I woke up in the morning and I was just thinking. Blue is the color you don't see anymore. Blue is from milk of magnesia bottles. Now they make milk of magnesia in plastic. There is blue beach glass in my jar.

NAN: I will look at my topless blender in the same light one day. I will never forgive myself for not remembering to take that top from the house.

65

MIE: Imagine all the wonderful thing lost in fire.

MICHELE: Imagine all the stupid things saved from fires—a children's book no one has heard of, a blender, beach glass.

> TIM *is inside the country house and gets up, because there are car lights outside, and a car stops in front of the house and a car door is heard opening and closing and footsteps are heard, and so* TIM *hides behind the door; in his hand, he holds the hammer. Door opens . . . Enter* JEAN.

JEAN: Roger? Roger?

> *(She walks past* TIM, *whom she can't see, then she goes into the kitchen, looks around, goes to the washing machine, and touches the hole in the washing machine.* TIM *walks into the kitchen behind her)*

TIM: It still runs.

JEAN *(Turning around)*: Where's your father?

TIM: I know. I did a load today.

JEAN: Is he sleeping?

TIM: I used this. *(Holding up hammer)* It is amazing what leverage is all about; the farther you hold it down on the handle, the harder it hits . . . Why are you here? You never come here? He's got a garden, you know. Brussels sprouts, I just learned, grow on stalks, twenty—thirty of them, all clinging to one stalk. And the bull, there's a bull out back.

JEAN: Did the bull do this?

TIM: There really is a brass ring inside the bull's nose, and you pull on that ring and he goes wild, but he follows behind you and you can lead him anywhere.

JEAN: You led the bull through here?

TIM: The bull lives in the field. Want to see him get mad? Go around the side of the fence and snort like he would snort; shake the bushes, he thinks you are there to get his cows.

JEAN *(Sitting)*: Is there anything to drink? *(*TIM *goes to the cupboard and takes out a cracked bottle of gin and pours her some in a dirty* *glass from the sink. She takes the glass and looks at it)* What if there's glass in here, Tim? *(But she drinks it, anyway)*

TIM *(Sitting across from her)*: This is a great house.

JEAN: Yeah? Why? *(She looks around)* It looks like Cain was raised in here . . . Yes, maybe it's a nice house. It's got those high beams.

TIM: Maybe I will do that next.

JEAN: What?

TIM: Saw a beam in half. The roof would then cave in.

JEAN: Why'd you do it, Tim?

TIM: I felt like it.

JEAN: He see it yet?

TIM: He heard about it. I called him on the phone.

JEAN: You lose a girl or something?

TIM: No. I just felt like it. I felt like making him think a little. He walks around here like nothing will ever happen. He leaves the door open; people, anybody can just walk in. He leaves the fire burning in the stove when he goes away for the day. His dog runs with no leash.

JEAN: He is afraid all of the time. I am the one who killed the black snake in the basement when he could not.

TIM: You can tell the men who sweat in their sleep and only in their sleep. *(JEAN lays her head down on the table)* Are you drunk, Mom?

JEAN: A little. I went out to dinner; I remember showing the guy I went out with how I could whistle with my fingers in my mouth, as if to catch a cab. I can't remember if he was impressed or not, but every waiter came up to our table afterward, refilling our water glasses, emptying our ashtray.

TIM: I didn't know you could do that. Do it again.

   (JEAN sticks her fingers in her mouth while she is still resting her head on the table)

JEAN: I can't. It was a once-in-a-lifetime thing.

TIM *(Getting up)*: I can do it with grass. A blade of grass. I'll show you. *(He exits)*

JEAN: Oh yeah, your father would do that all the time, stick a blade of grass between his fingers as if he was making the church, oh, I mean the steeple. *(She starts doing this, saying to herself . . .)* This is the church, this is the steeple, open the doors and see all the people. This is the church, this is the steeple, open the doors and see all the people.

   (TIM comes running in, banging the door behind him and locking it, then running behind JEAN)

TIM: It's after me! He thought I was after his cows. He jumped the fence, he bowed his head to the ground, he stamped his foot, he threw up his tail. *(He goes to the window, moves the curtain aside to look out)* If he were here, he would leave the door open, let the bull run in.

JEAN: He might do it *(She joins TIM at the window)*—leave the door open, but he would run up onto the counter to watch the bull . . . Funny, you can't tell the bull is there; except you can't see part of the fence, as if your father forgot to build that part of the fence.

TIM: Or he left that part of the fence open, wanting things to storm through his land and into his house.

JEAN: That bull has it easy. He does not say he wants to come in, he just knows he has to get in. He does not come to ask for the man of the house. He does not have to tell us his name. *(TIM puts a chair on the countertop and then climbs up to the beam in the center of the kitchen and sits on the beam. JEAN sits on the countertop)* Tell me how you lost this girl. She go with someone else?

TIM: I did not lose a girl. *(He lies down on the beam)* This is not about a girl . . . Mom, from up here the kitchen does not look so bad.

JEAN: When your father left, I went up to the Empire State Building to look out.

TIM: Did you feel better?

JEAN: I tried to find our house, but I could not, so then I realized that if I could not find our house, I would never be able to see you or your father, so I felt his leaving was just a small thing, but my children—I became sad when I knew I could not see you all the way down there. You are my mark in this world.

TIM: You want to come up here with me?

JEAN: I ran home. I got inside and I picked up Nan, even though she was too big for picking up and her legs dragged on the floor when I kissed her. *(She begins to clear the things off the countertop, so that she can lie down. She seems drunker)* You tell your father when he comes in that I wanted to talk to him. No, that's not true, I wanted to see him. I want to look at him and think how I don't love him anymore. You know, he was the one who taught me how to whistle like that. One day we sat and learned, and he put his fingers into my mouth to show me how and where to put my tongue. *(She drifts off)*

TIM: Mom? Mom? I don't know when he'll be back. The house is on fire. *(He gets off the beam, takes a tablecloth and covers his sleeping mother with it, then goes into the next room and comes back with a saw, begins to climb back up to the beam. While he is doing all this, he is saying)* Ladybug, ladybug, fly away home, your house is on fire, your children are gone—Ladybug, ladybug, fly away home.

Back at the churchyard.

ROGER: She is probably in there sleeping through this whole thing and she is too lazy to get out of bed. I have never known a grown woman to sleep so much. She would stay in bed until five o'clock in the afternoon. It is a strange feeling to spend the whole day at work, then come home to find the curtains still drawn and your wife still sleeping. It makes you feel as if you have done nothing all day. I would stay later at work. I would get home so late she would be back in bed already, that is, if she had gotten up at all, and it was better that way for a while, because I could imagine all the things she had done during the day. It is not right to wish upon your wife an affair—to sleep with another man just so you can say my wife at least does something; that she really does not sleep all day.

MIE: Yes, you were always a great believer in affair. Doesn't it renew the soul, enhance the sex life with the married partner, bring an element of danger so very close that it is exciting?

ROGER: It will not take long for this house to burn down to the ground.

MIE: And the old amah keeps thinking she sees you on television, because you look like that doctor man. For so long we have told her no, that you are not playing a doctor, but she still believes it, and then some day who wants to tell her no; maybe it is better for her to believe that you are doing something worthwhile, maybe her believing so hard makes us believe it, too.

NAN: I will believe the blender top is still here.

MICHELE: You cannot do that with the ring.

MIE: I gave the ring to your mother. You have given the ring to the fire. The fire will give it back.

ROGER: Don't tell my children lies.

MIE: So we keep telling the old amah yes, and she goes up to the television and she touches the face of the doctor she thinks is you.

NAN: Do you realize our mother has still not come home?

MICHELE: The slut.

NAN: The bimbo.

ROGER: If this were my house, and I saw it burning from far away, I would not come home either.

MICHELE: When it is all over, will the men let us walk through the smoking debris?

ROGER: After my fire, there was nothing to keep except a metal glass my father took from a Pullman train years ago.

MICHELE: Do you still have the glass?

ROGER: I set it in the windowsill in the country.

NAN: You don't know what Tim's done to that glass.

MICHELE: This is when we go ask the firemen if we can go in and see.

NAN: This is when I say, let me in, open wide your pockets, fork up my blender top.

MICHELE: This is when we find our mother sleeping in a pillowcase.

(The girls drop their blankets from their shoulders and leave. ROGER picks up their blankets and begins to fold them. MIE drinks more. It is easy to see she is becoming very drunk)

MIE: You take those blanket and someone will know. All those dead people with their skin stuck to those blanket, they will know, they will come back to get you. Your children will come back wanting those blanket, wanting to make tepee with those blanket, hang those blanket over tree wanting to get under those blanket and you will have hidden those blanket from them.

ROGER: You never had a ring from Marie Antoinette. Why didn't you tell her that, in the car, on the ice?

MIE: You cannot tell me that ring was not from Marie Antoinette.

ROGER: For years now, she has had that ring and has let her children try it on.

MIE: How do you know that metal cup your father had was taken from a Pullman train?

ROGER: Because he told me.

MIE: Maybe he just told you that so you would think of him for the rest of your life, that after he died you would still have the cup, do what you have done with it: kept it, gone back for it after fires. It could have been anything. It could have been eyeglass, a book, a ring.

ROGER: Only a selfish person would do that.

MIE: What my father told me was a ghost story. Long ago, a woman lived and died, but she came back to torment the people that moved into her house after her death and every night she would try to claw with her fingernail through the thatch roof of the house. Every night after the family went to bed, they would hear the clawing on the roof, and then they would hear the drop of blood from her finger, as she tried to claw through the roof, drip down onto the ground. My father would tell that ghost story every time that it rained, saying the rain was the woman's blood. Every time that it rains, I think of my father.

ROGER: So your father gave you the rain?

MIE: And your father gave you the cup and I gave my daughter the ring.

ROGER: And the girls will think of their mother every time they think of the ring or of the fire or of Marie Antoinette?

(Enter the girls, holding firemen hats)

MICHELE: They would not let us in, but they gave us these to wear.

ROGER *(Reaching out for a hat)*: They gave you these hats? Don't give these hats back; these hats are not made out of plastic, these hats are made of tempered steel; you wear these hats in a hailstorm and you can go about your business.

MICHELE: They say it is almost over.

NAN: They say the beams have fallen in. They say it is a blessing. They say it is as if God has put His finger on a knot while tying a bow, and the beams, like the bow, has fallen in.

MICHELE: They say this to everyone.

ROGER: I have seen hailstones the size of golf balls dent the hoods of cars.

MIE: Here everything is the size of something else. The size of an orange, the size of a golf ball, the size of a melon, the size of two head. Nothing is what it is in this country. **Q**

What Do You Have to Do?

Saldi saw food carts with trays of food, spilled milk, uneaten beans; blue fluorescent tubing flickered overhead. From some of the rooms came the nervous light of television. Saldi carried the sense that he shouldn't be here. He was an interloper, an intruder. The day had ended: his presence was extending the day.

The guard checked the number on the door. "The gentleman dying in there is your father?"

"Yes."

"Be swift. Lingering reminds them of death."

Saldi peered into the room. The television screen showed a hospital room. People were gathered about a hospital bed. Saldi's father, hair messed, eyes closed, head slumped forward, snored weakly, half asleep. Saldi stayed in the hallway. He wondered if it was the guard who had telephoned him. They called regularly now. "Come quick," they said. But they were always wrong.

The weeping hour: ancient minds remembered griefs a half century old; silent tear-fall permeated the building. The tired bodies were vulnerable to forgotten emotions, regretted joys. The evening was the worst hour: the sun was gone, daylight thinned, breezes moved through the wet leaves.

Like a transatlantic ocean liner, the nursing home displayed an information board that indicated the day of the week, the month, the year, and the current state of the weather. Old people gathered daily to stare at it with glaucomatous eyes:

Saturday
May 29, 1982
Sunny and Clear

Saldi read it, rainwater puddling on the floor as it dripped from his coat and umbrella.

On the door to his father's room was a chart Saldi read regularly. The medical staff measured the amount of fluids put into his father and measured the amount of fluids that emerged from him, and each day, like contest results, the winning figures were posted on the door for everybody to see.

"My, he's certainly peeing well," a bald, aged woman told Saldi. Saldi was ashamed of the revulsion he felt at these old people. He wished them all to be young again. Is there any visitor to a nursing home who isn't reminded that he may end his years there?

In the room, the halls, the stairwell, the smell of urine was all-pervading, dominating: urine in sheets, urine in rugs, urine on walls, old urine, fresh urine, the urine of the long-departed (their legacy on earth), white urine, yellow urine, urine from old incontinent pudenda filled the home and filled Saldi's father's small room.

Saldi moved a *Time* magazine to a clear spot on the dresser and placed on it the warm potato salad he had brought with him. For a moment the fragrance of potatoes and vinegar filled the air. His father woke, an absent look on his face, hair wild as feathers, smiling a smile that Saldi saw often, a smile that demonstrated a certain cavalier ambiguity. People who suffer ambiguities were weeded out early in the legal profession: Saldi's father never rose beyond the county bench. After his stroke, the ambiguity became more intense. Sitting beside the bed in the nursing home, Saldi turned his head so the tears wouldn't show when his father spoke. "Our seed will prosper here, Marty. Our seed will own condos and Audis. We'll have smart seed."

"How is he?" Saldi would sometimes ask Dr. Corless.

"Not good. He walks some. But he's dying at a healthier rate now."

Saldi helped his father to the bathroom. His father leaned against him as he pissed and shat, and Saldi could feel his father's bones and thin muscles. He helped clean his father. Mucus rattled in his father's throat; his mind seemed to wander down a garden path of his own planting. He spoke, remembering legal maxims that came to his mind, remembering parts of cases he had tried, remembering defendants he had sent to jail.

"I sent eighteen Richards to jail. Only four Steves," he said. "One Louise."

Maybe his father had known what was awaiting him. Toward the end of his career, he volunteered to serve on two civic committees whose purpose was to force modernization of nursing homes. None of the proposed legislation was successful. Now it was too late. He was thinner now, smaller, shorter, like the other inhabitants of the home, quietly shrinking to coffin size, becoming tinier, so that there was less of them that had to die.

Lucid moments: "How's that damned priest Rotter?"

"Fine," Saldi said.

"His Death Consolation Group?"

"Fine."

"They never *have* prevented anyone from dying."

"They're just a volunteer group, Dad. No funding."

His father turned his head, unsatisfied.

Saldi remembered that his father had never showed displeasure at home. He had been patient with him. When Saldi was a child, his father used to stand on his head, and pennies and nickels would drop out of his pants pocket. Saldi dived for the nickels with a whoop.

"Did I ever own a Chevrolet?"

"Yes, Dad."

"Did we have a courthouse?"

"Yes, Dad."

His father closed his eyes and seemed to consider this

piece of information. He concentrated. Saldi imagined that this datum sat at the very forefront of his father's brain. You could almost see it.

"Did the courthouse get many miles to the gallon?" his dad asked.

Saldi patted his father's hand.

His father frowned, then spoke: "Courthouses are those big buildings with cafeterias in the basement, aren't they? I remember lots of ham sandwiches and handcuffed niggers."

"Yes, Dad. That's a courthouse."

"There's a wonderful rhythm to the place. In the late afternoons, the courtrooms and corridors empty. People on the fringes of the criminal justice system leave then, carrying their lunch baskets and newspapers."

His dad was silent for a moment, and then he nodded his head, as if he knew what he was thinking about. He turned to Saldi with a surprised look on his face. It was clear that a new piece of information had taken up residence in the forefront of his brain.

"Do I have to do anything for death?" his father asked.

Saldi said nothing. Then: "Death?"

"Do I have to do anything?" his father asked.

Saldi remained silent.

"Well, do I?"

"No," Saldi said.

"Do I sign any papers?"

"Not required."

Saldi's father looked unsure, suspicious.

"Whom do I have to tell?" he asked.

"No one."

"Where do I get permission?"

"Nowhere."

"How many documents are there?"

"None."

"Who has to know?"

"Nobody."

"How much does it cost?"

"It's free."

"Who pays for it?"

"It's taken care of."

"I don't want to owe anybody."

"Don't worry about it, Dad."

"Don't be ridiculous," his father said, settling back on the pillow. "Everybody worries about death."

Saldi's mother had once complained to him: All the damn Saldis were the same. They were bright—you could see it in their eyes—and they performed well at college. They began careers well; they made friends easily. Then, poof: something happened to them when they reached their thirties, something no one liked. They cut back on exertions; they no longer seemed to compete. They spotted some glitch in life that gave them pause.

Saldi suspected that, between them, he and his father had the will to survive of a single person. Together, Saldi and his father had the ability to get through a single normal life. As far as Saldi could tell, the will to get on with things could be flipped on and off like a light switch. He didn't know who flipped the switch. When it was off, neither would budge from his bed; they saw no glory in consciousness, unwilling to eat, to stand up, to work. Saldi's father had been the worst. He shat and pissed in bed. Food had to be brought to him. The room smelled. There was nothing to be done but wait it out. Gradually, whatever it was within him that had opened his eyes to such a malevolent existence would fade away and Saldi's father would become active and half-alert, and he'd slink back into the world. While at the same time, Saldi would be subsiding.

Saldi knew what was coming, and he knew he could do nothing to prevent it. He sank into depression, sleeping and drinking bad Lipton tea on the couch, watching steam rise from the cup in the sunlight. His mind was crowded with thoughts he wasn't responsible for. Days passed like this, as if there was no reason they shouldn't. Then, without warning, the switch would be flipped, and like his father, he would begin to emerge from his despondency and attend to his daily needs. Who knew what it all meant?

Saldi's father began snoring. Saldi walked to the corridor, where the smell was not as bad. Saldi still had to discuss with his father cleaning out the basement in the family home, where thirty years of clothes and books and photographs had accumulated. How was Saldi going to clean the basement? Where was he going to store the boxes of clothes and the old Lionel train that was still, thirty years after construction, mounted on a wooden table, with tunnels and mountains and siding and switches. Saldi's father possessed trunks of old bank statements, insurance policies that Saldi would have to review, law books, memoranda, opinions. What did his father want to do with them?

The train had been Saldi's. He loved it. If he placed small white pills in the smokestack, the engine gave out smoke that trailed over the tracks and snuck through the tunnels. He could load magnetic cattle onto cattle cars with the push of a button. He could make men in blue overalls wave red lanterns. With a flip of a switch, he began the world; with a flip of a switch, he turned it off.

Saldi stared into his father's room. One of the women on television knelt by the bed. Saldi stepped back from the doorway. He saw himself in the small mirror next to the drinking fountain. Collar frayed, cuffs frayed. He sipped warm water that dripped from his chin. God, it was easy to deteriorate.

A quick look in the mirror. The skin beneath Saldi's eyes was no better than his cuffs: if he were ten years older, his situation would be suicidal. He knew if he got the train going at a certain speed, he could make it jump the tracks and fall to the floor. He toyed with that again and again, tempting disaster. One night, he turned up the transformer and watched the locomotive fall like lead to the floor. Tiny wheels and screws scattered like spiders across the cement. He told his father it was an accident. His father took the locomotive to a hobby shop. Parts had to be sent for. Weeks went by when Saldi could not run the world he loved. When the locomotive was returned to the tracks, it rested at an angle and never ran as well as formerly. The heating element that produced the smoke couldn't be repaired.

"Your father passed away?"

Saldi looked up, surprised. A man in a white medical coat and trimmed blond beard with an odor of after-shave was standing beside him. He held out pink sheets of Kleenex. Saldi took them and wiped at the tears on his cheeks.

"He was wonderful. A character. A delight," the man said softly. "Go ahead. Confront the grief you feel."

Saldi blew his nose on the Kleenex and stared at the man, who smiled comfortingly at him.

The man spoke in a quiet, measured voice. "Catharsis accompanies the loss of a loved one. These are feelings that are shared by the entire race of man. Let the tears flow. Feelings make brothers of us all." He put a manicured hand on Saldi's shoulder and gave a little pat. "More tears are shed in this hallway than in any other hallway on earth."

The man looked past Saldi into the room. "I'll turn off the television."

"He's watching it," Saldi said.

The man stared at Saldi. "Then why are you crying?"

Saldi shook his head. There were swamps of sadness in the nursing home: all around were the people who had failed to tap into the really good gene pools. It was a place where you could not enjoy your own father's last days.

"You shouldn't be crying in this hallway."

Saldi stared at the doctor. Was he a doctor? Saldi saw that the man's left eye was bad, and when he wanted to look at you, he turned his head so that the right eye could see you. Apparently the man's right ear was deaf, and when Saldi spoke to him, he swiveled his head so that his left ear was closest to Saldi. While they spoke, the man's head swiveled back and forth as if he was disagreeing with everything Saldi said.

"Your father is coughing at us."

Saldi and the doctor went into the room.

His father sat up. "What am I going to do?"

"About what?"

"About my things."

"Draft a will," Saldi said.

"You said papers weren't required."

"Place your real property in joint tenancy."

"You said I didn't need any documents."

"Transfer personal possessions to heirs."

"Transfer personal possessions to heirs?"

"Through gifts."

"Gifts?"

"That's a start."

"Why is it a start?"

"Don't you want to avoid probate?"

"I want to avoid death."

The doctor's head was watching, listening, swiveling, swiveling, negative, negation, denial, rebuttal.

"You said I didn't need to do those things."

"Dad, I was just saying those things."

"Why did you say them?"

"We've got to keep lying to you, Dad."

"How much longer are you going to lie to me?"

"Only about another week or so," the doctor said.

The father stared at his son. They had the same pattern of wrinkles stamped on their faces. Another thirty years and Saldi would be the one in the bed.

A black nurse eating fish and chips watched the security guard unlock the door and allow Saldi to exit. "I'll telephone if there is a change in condition," the guard said.

Saldi smelled vinegar as he left the building. **Q**

My Boy's Girl

I've got to get this off my chest before I start. I want
you to know that I have never been able to do much with my
boy. Even when he was quite a small child, I couldn't do much
with him: I could never even catch him to spank him. He could
always run faster than I, so you can imagine what it was like
later on. He's the wall type, if you see what I mean: stubborn.
Besides, if you really think about it, who of us has been able
to do anything with our children?

Now, where to start? I suppose with the Italian. The Italian
will do as well as anything. I suppose you could say—arbitrar-
ily, of course—that the thing started, as so many things have,
with the Italian.

There was a soft breeze from the sea the day the Italian arrived in the rooms we rent on the top floor of this house,
with the terrace on the garden side and not facing the sea. The
rooms have wicker furniture and faded cretonne curtains,
paper-thin walls, and slippery tiled floors that shake a little and
squeak as you walk, the sand from the beach beneath your feet.
We took the rooms because of the garden, and because of the
price. My alimony, you know, comes in dollars, and the dollar,
just then, was rather weak. As it turned out, the landlord never
gave us the key to the iron gate of the closed garden, and we
can only stand, enviously, looking down into the well of shiny
tropical plants and lush green shade, with the scent of mag-
nolias rising up to us on our terrace in the heat.

A charming boy, the Italian, I thought, with his black hair
brushed neatly back from his high forehead, his white linen
suit, his elaborate manners, and in his hand a leather-bound
book. We sat on the terrace sipping cool drinks at dusk, the
boy's pale forehead glimmering in the half-light. I asked questions. I'm good at that. He and my boy talked.

What the Italian talked about was this girl he had met by chance in Rome. He said the girl owned diamond mines, so many diamond mines, and shook out his long white fingers from the wrist, like money, it seemed to me, falling from trees. He was not sure what the girl was actually doing in Rome, or what had brought her and her family from their lonely home in some vast wilderness to the Eternal City. The Italian said the family had a furnished apartment in Rome, with a Watteau clown in white, a table with magnificent butterflies in phosphorescent blues and blacks pressed under glass, and a maid who spoke no known language, who followed the girl like a shadow wherever she walked. He said the girl studied Italian with a private tutor, crossing the river to go to the tutor's small, shuttered flat, where the tutor sat intoning Dante fervently, tears in her eyes, a hand on her bosom, a shadow of dark hair on her top lip.

As the Italian was talking, I watched him fingering the leaves of the leather-bound volume, a gift, he told us, from this girl, something old and quite unreadable, I thought; Corneille, or perhaps it was Racine. I watched as the Italian turned the fine pages of the book, and the breeze blew, the scent of magnolia rising in the air, a photograph fluttering to the floor, where it lay in the dust.

The boys bent to pick up the photograph, knocking heads, the dark against the blond. I noticed that it was my boy who clasped the photograph in his hand and lifted it up to the fading light. My boy said, "Not bad," shrugging his shoulders with apparent nonchalance and then handing it over to me.

I said, "Very pretty, indeed," and nodded appreciatively at the Italian. What else could I do?

Now, I want you to know that, before my boy left for Rome, I said to him, lifting an ancient Chinese vase, a gift from a lover—there have been a few of those—into the air, "If you steal that boy's girl, I'll break this thing over your head." We laughed, and of course, he set out to do exactly that. As I said before, there was never much I could do with my boy.

What happened in Rome I can only surmise. This is how I see it: The Italian is standing in the shadows of some Baroque church, waving his fingers at a dark painting elegantly. He speaks volubly, offering up what he has to offer: his ancient city, his culture, his love of art. The Italian says, "Look at the line of that shoulder. Look how it flows."

I see the girl beside the Italian, in a white dress with a high collar and a billowy skirt. She has that pallor tinged with carmine in her cheeks. The girl's transparent eyes wander from the line of the Madonna's shoulder to the window above. The girl watches a swallow drift like a windblown leaf across the sky. Or perhaps she stares at a beam of light on the stone floor. She does not look at my boy, who stands near her, long and loose-limbed, his white shirt-sleeves turned back to the bony elbows, a blond forelock in his eyes. He gazes avidly at the girl with his acquisitive glance, taking in the long neck and the swell of the breasts.

I can only presume that the glances had little or no effect, for the girl departed one night, went off wordlessly with her mother and aunt, drifted northward, so my boy said. Who knows why? Perhaps the girl went northward for the music, for the vista from the castle, which is, they say, splendid, or perhaps for want of anything better to do.

What happened next my boy described to me over the telephone. He told me how he had followed the girl, in hot pursuit, as he said, driving all night in the rain without even knowing where the girl was to stay, because she had left no address behind or, if she had left one, it was with the Italian, and the Italian was not giving out any addresses of that kind.

My boy told me how he had roamed the city, checking all the best hotels, thinking that would be where the girl would stay, but spotting her finally, hours later, not in any hotel, but walking down the street, making her way absently through the crowd. He said the rain had stopped and the sun was shining, glistening on wet pavement and summer leaves. The top to his car was down as he saw the girl in the throng of tourists in the street. He jammed on the brakes, stood up, he said, dropping the wheel and shouting out her name wildly. The girl turned and stared. What the girl was doing, my boy told me, was looking for tickets to hear a diva sing *Così Fan Tutte.*

The next I heard, they were married. I do not know how my boy managed this. Perhaps, quite simply, he got her with child, or he might have said something that pleased her momentarily. Perhaps he had said that he liked French literature more than he did Russian, or Russian more than French. Perhaps he took her driving in the dim forest that surrounds that city and, in the gloaming, with the scent of pine in the air, stopped his car suddenly and turned to her, hitting her in the eye with one of those bony elbows, and the girl, momentarily blinded, may have thought: Well, why not? The girl may have thought, Why not this long, loose-limbed American with the golden forelock, rather than the dark Italian with the ancient culture, after all? Perhaps she thought: What difference would it make anyway in the end? Perhaps she thought that marriage, like death, was inevitable. Perhaps she thought the rich could afford to be careless.

One thing I know is that she was not in love with my boy. It was quite obvious to me as they walked through the door at the end of the summer for a visit, my boy pushing his prize before him proudly, that baby grin spreading wide as all the world. One look at the girl in a narrow, dark blue dress, idly eyeing the magnolia tree and twisting her triple string of pearls around her delicate fingers, and I could see.

She had the static, anonymous prettiness of a porcelain doll. The head appeared too heavy for the slender neck, the big eyes blinked blankly, aquamarine; the teeth glimmered blue-white. She lacked something, it was obvious to me, but I was not certain what. It seemed to me that some sort of gauzy veil hung between her and the rest of humanity. What I thought it was, at first—the veil, that is—was simply stupidity. I was wrong about that. Later, I imagined she had suffered some loss in her early years. At times, it even occurred to me that she had inherited some fatal strain of fragility that would impair my boy's life.

Day after day, they lingered on in the rooms at the top of the house, as the summer waned. Increasingly uneasy, I began to see that they had little intention of moving on, though my boy was due back at school. Indeed, my boy seemed less and less capable of moving anywhere. When I asked, "What about the future?" or "What about your degree?" he shrugged his shoulders and told me he was taking a "love sabbatical," that he was in no hurry, that they needed nothing, that there was nothing to worry about, and went out with the girl to buy sweet cakes for our tea.

The girl, if she had ever been with child, was no longer so. If any new life had sprung up within her narrow form, it had flickered out fast. I saw no signs of swelling there. Like the head, the body seemed doll-like to me, irrevocably locked within its white skin, narrow hips, slight childlike curve of stomach, straight stiff legs.

I do not mean to imply that the girl was silent, for that she was certainly not. It was rather as though she had no idea of what to keep to herself and what not. At times, she babbled on quite recklessly about her childhood in that savage place, describing with much detail the old rambling house with the courtyards, the verandas, the mango and avocado trees; and about her family, numerous unmarried uncles and aunts, cousins, hangers-on, servants, and even the household pets—there was a monkey, I believe, or some such thing, and a brightly colored parrot she had once owned who kept saying, "Watch out! Watch out! Watch out for thieves!"

At other moments she drifted barefoot past me across the tiled floors, as though I did not exist at all. She wandered through the rooms indolently, letting her clothes lie where they fell, shutting herself up in the bath for hours, reading Proust. Afterward, I found the volume facedown on the tiles, the pages wet.

Sometimes, at twilight, she would appear at the front door, her cheeks flushed with the effort of the climb up the stairs, her arms full of flowers from the market in the town. She would lay out newspaper on the kitchen table and stand before the big glass bowl, carefully arranging the blooms. There were snapdragons, tulips, yellow roses, daisies, baby's breath, and sometimes an orchid or two.

Arranging flowers seemed all she knew how to do. Once, I asked her to help me prepare an evening meal. I stared at her as she stood obligingly at the sink, turning on the taps fast and watching as the water cascaded onto the lettuce, bruising the leaves. After dinner, she sat out on the terrace, gazing up at the stars. It seemed to me that the mosquitoes that devoured everyone else left her alone.

I found myself watching her increasingly on the beach. She went down to the sea in the heat of the day and lay for a while, half-naked, curled up in the shade. I watched her as she rose and climbed the dunes, picking the white wildflowers, the lilies that grew in the long grass, filling glass vases later with flowers that faded fast.

Like some sea creature, static, almost awkward on land, she seemed to come alive in the water, diving from rocks, her body trembling, her skin glistening, her back curving as she entered the water, like a lacquered bud. I strained my eyes to see her as she struck out for the horizon, beating straight arms and legs fearlessly, and then, tiring perhaps, letting a wave catch her up, roll her and twist her, and throw her onto the sand, where she lay like some castaway from a strange land.

At night, I was awakened by the sound of someone moving about, drifting through the rooms. In dreams, I saw the girl, a ghostlike figure standing at the iron gate of the garden, her hands on the bars. One night, I awoke to hear the sound of her voice calling out my boy's name with what I thought was fear. I heard her sob and say, "It's so dark in here."

As the days passed, and the mists rose, covering the beach, the sea, and the sky, I heard my boy's voice rise gradually. Through the thin walls, I heard him pacing up and down with long, impatient steps. One morning I heard him shout, "Oh shit! What's the matter with you, anyway?" And once I think he said, "Why can't you, for Christ's sake? Why can't you?" Or was it, "Why not, in Christ's name, why not?" I heard objects fall and shatter on the floor. Once, I thought I heard the sound of a blow: a hand against a head.

In the evenings, when the crowds had left the beach, my boy and I sometimes walked together across the sand. We stopped to admire the sun setting across the water, the sea and the sky lit up with the colors of a dying conflagration. My boy would disclose very little, however much I pressed. He just walked beside me, silently, his long arms swinging and his head beating back and forth, back and forth, like a metronome keeping time to his steps. Sometimes I would tire, sit for a while, and my boy would take off, running down the beach, wheeling, and then coming back to me.

One misty evening, he said more than he usually did, though what he said was not exactly clear to me. I suppose I was going on about his making plans to get back to school. He mumbled, I believe, "I'm not sure what to do about her." I think I asked if there was something wrong; was there, perhaps, some problem between the two of them?

I looked at the gray of the sea and sky, at the bare branches of trees like the veins of a hand. Perhaps I made some suggestion. One tries to help, after all. I may have suggested an occupation of some kind, or a doctor's advice, a stay in some clinic specializing in things of the sort.

"Easier said than done," he may have mumbled in reply. That's another thing about my boy: he never speaks clearly, but talks to his toes, if you know what I mean. I'm always telling him to stand to his full height. He's a good height, you know, takes after me in that way, but he stoops, hangs his head, and mumbles like that, especially just when you want to hear what he says. I suppose I asked, panting a little, trying to catch up with him, my feet sinking into the sand, "Do you love her?"

"Oh, love," he said impatiently, running ahead a little way, turning to me, his back to the light, pulling the hood of his shirt over his hair, flapping his long arms at his side. From afar he said something that sounded to me like "Oh, no, love's not the problem. It's life."

I saw them off at the station in early December. They were standing there, stamping cold feet in the mist. As the train drew in, I turned to the girl and held her close to me. She was muffled in a white fur coat with a white fur hat drawn down over her pale eyes. I said, "Darling, do take care," and brushed my lips against her cheek, her skin smooth and cold, her perfume thin and sweet. She drew back. For a moment I clung to the fur of her coat. I watched as she turned away and climbed the steps of the train slowly, with what seemed a certain solemnity. She seemed grave, almost sad. My boy followed with his long, impatient strides.

I walked slowly up all those stairs to empty rooms, where I waited anxiously for news. When it came, though, when the letter came eventually, my boy was writing to say that he was back in school, that his studies were going on successfully, that they had found a place to stay, and that the girl was with child. Despite this, in the months that followed and all through the spring and summer of the year, I continued to think of the girl almost ceaselessly, with something approaching fear. When I walked the beach in the bright light at noon, catching a glimpse of a white back, or of long dark hair dripping beads of water, or of a diver about to plunge into the sea, then, for a moment, I thought of her and of my boy. But the vision was always unclear.

SHEILA KOHLER

White light streamed in under the arcades as I walked
down the main street of the town early, going out as I usually
do for my newspaper and bun. The palm fronds beat with a
dry sound in the breeze that blew from the glittering sea. The
place seemed colorless, bleached, without character, planted
there without reason, or if there had once been a reason, it was
no longer apparent to me, or not apparent at this time of year.
Even the few people in the street seemed to wander about
somewhat aimlessly, calling to one another from time to time,
without hurrying, as though the streets were not there for the
business of living but only as a place to pass through. I
thought: A day for the terrace with a blanket on the knees and
perhaps a walk on the beach.

I prepared my breakfast as I do each morning; the bun, the
boiled egg, the coffee with the beaten milk were on the terrace
on a tray. The telephone rang. It was my boy, weeping on the
phone. I could hardly hear what he was saying over and over
again, but it was not necessary for me to hear. There was
nothing I could say: I could not tell him his news was hardly
a surprise to me. Finally, I said, "Darling, you'd best come
home soon," and put down the telephone. I walked out onto
the terrace and looked down into the closed garden below,
staring into the well of shiny tropical plants and lush green
shade. The light in the leaves seemed very bright to me, the
blue of the empty sky perfect. Then I sat down and ate my
breakfast methodically.

One must keep up one's strength. **Q**

Clips

I want you with only your skirt on, the man says. The woman begins to take off her things and the man stops her. No, I want you to leave your top slip on. Nothing else. So you will look like someone who is in a department store trying on clothes. The woman reaches under her slip and unhooks her bra. Now take off your shoes and remove your stockings, the man says. And stand over here, on this small rug. The woman takes off her shoes and stockings. You are not wearing lipstick, the man says. You must wear lipstick that is a dark color. I want you to paint your lips black. The woman takes something from her purse. The man says, I want you to put more rouge on your cheeks, underneath your cheekbones, so that your face looks heavy and wide. Now take off your clothes, all your clothes, and lie across the bed with a book in your hand, as if you are going to read something. The man hands the woman a book from the dresser. No, you have it entirely wrong, he says. You are wearing too much makeup and your eyes look like the eyes of an old woman. The woman goes to the bathroom and she removes her makeup. I cannot make love to you like this, the man says. You must turn over so it is not possible for me to see your face except in the bureau mirror. Turn over so all I can see is your back. Now put a blanket over yourself and then take the blanket off, like this. Take the blanket off as if it is summer and the room is very warm. As if it is very warm inside the room and you are about to shower. As you get up from the bed, I will take you from behind, with your hair hanging loose and without clips. You must twist around, like this, the man says. As if you are going to turn completely. The woman takes the clips from her hair and her hair falls to her shoulders. Now you must dress, the man says. And leave me. **Q**

The Mascot

My mother had been acting strange since the Hallow-een when she dressed up like a gorilla for work. After that, my mother kept wearing the head of her gorilla suit. She did not wear the gorilla head all the time, only once in a while. Sometimes, when I got up in the morning, my mother would be sitting in the kitchen and she would have on her gorilla head. I would talk to her, and she would take off her gorilla head and talk to me, and then she would put the gorilla head back on again.

"Can you do anything for your depression?" I said.

"I can take drugs," she said.

I watched half of my mother's throat swallowing while she finished her coffee. Then she got up and fixed meat patties for us. I watched my mother rolling the round meat patties with her hands. Then she put the patties on the broiling pan inside the oven. While the meat patties were cooking, my mother fed the cat. By the way, in the morning, my mother ate her muffin on a napkin, and it seemed to me that she thought that we were visiting in our apartment, and that it was her job to try to make the place look as if no one had been there, for when the real people came home. Anyway, when my mother finished eating her meat patty, she drank her Fresca from the can. I went to my room and I could hear her clipping around in her high heels. I tried to imagine my mother meeting someone in one of her night classes and getting married. I thought that, even with a husband, my mother would bring him coffee in a Styro-foam cup. I think that the only change would be with the gorilla head, that she would either take it off or put back on the whole suit. **Q**

Mexicans

My father said that I should not marry a Mexican. If I married a Mexican, my father said, I would have to take a big fat smelly Mexican family around with me everywhere I went. All the big fat sweaty lazy filthy Mexican aunts and uncles and grandparents, and all the dirty ragged no-good rotten stinking Mexican kids. If I married a Mexican, my father said, I would have fat oily smelly babies that would become short stupid good-for-nothing loud-mouthed ignorant Mexicans. My back yard would always be filled with packs of dirty grimy filthy Mexicans and my bathtub would be covered with thick brown filthy Mexican crud, with big black oily Mexican hairs stuck to everything. When I went somewhere in a car, the car would be packed full of hot fat stupid stinking Mexicans, so you could not breathe or see out the windows. How would I like that? My father said. Just how did I think I would like that? My father had a fistfight with a Mexican in our front yard, and my sister and I watched from the window. The Mexican did not fight back and my father split the man's big fat flat brown Mexican nose down the middle, so that it looked like a river with sand on both sides. Then my father came in the house and we could smell the rotten angry old canned-fish smell of my father. My father drew a chalk line on the sidewalk and whoever crossed over to the Mexican side got the shit beat out of them. We used to sit in the back yard and listen to the stupid fat ignorant know-nothing slimy Mexicans yelling out things next door. We could even hear the little kids talking fat stupid ugly slow lazy Mexican talk. My father said that Mexicans sat with their legs wide open and let everything just hang out right in your face for you to look at. When my sister got knocked up by one of the fat dirty stinking grimy Mexican workers that my father almost killed, we moved away. The baby was a girl, and you should have seen the way my father bounced that fat dark oily curly-haired Mexican girl on his back, making her laugh until she cried, so that her thick wet black Mexican curls got stuck close around her head like a small knitted cap. **Q**

Turbot, Tomossa

In a small village near the coast of Italy, there was a young girl who was plain and simple by nature. When the girl turned sixteen, her mother showed her how to prepare a noonday meal of baked turbot fillets. The girl was then married off to a local farmer. From the beginning, nothing but good fortune came to the young couple. The farmer planted and fertilized his crops, and his vegetables grew in abundance. Every morning, the farmer's wife carried a basket of produce to the market, and she returned with two fresh white turbot fillets. The farmer's wife prepared the noonday meal, exactly as her mother had shown her, and then she went to the garden and called to her husband. "Turbot, Tomossa," the girl said. The farmer rose from his crops, and he came to the table. The turbot fillets were fresh and lean, and they gave the farmer the strength to return to his crops, working until dark. One day, as the farmer's wife was preparing the noonday meal, a beautiful young woman came to the door. The woman said that she was the wife of the man who was building the large structure next to the farmer's cottage. The woman said that she had more money than she could spend, and she asked the farmer's wife to take some of her money. The farmer's wife looked around the small modest cottage, and she thought for a few moments before she replied. "I have no need of money," the farmer's wife said. "Then you will accept other gifts," the woman said. She took the farmer's wife's hand, and she ran it along the silk lining inside her jacket. "I have no need of gifts," the farmer's wife said. "Then let me show you how to prepare a feast that will make your husband happier than ever," the woman said. The farmer's wife looked out the window at her husband, who was bent over his crops. "Tomorrow," she replied. The next morning, the beautiful woman arrived at the cottage with bags of ingredients that the farmer's wife had never heard of. There were herbs and spices from far-off lands, and the woman mixed them in colorful pots and bowls. When the feast was spread upon the table, the woman said the name of the new meal, and the farmer's wife, having little else on her mind than the task at hand, repeated the word precisely. The farmer's wife then went to the garden and, instead of calling out, "Turbot, Tomossa," as she always had, she pronounced the new word. The farmer laid his tools in the dirt, but stayed crouched over his crops. The farmer's wife called again to her husband, but the farmer continued with his work. The next day, it was the same. After several days had passed, the farmer's wife prepared the noonday feast for her husband, and when she went to the garden, she found the farmer lying in the soil next to his vegetables. The farmer's wife was weary, and she lay down next to her husband and fell into a deep sleep. The structure next to the farmer's cottage continued to grow, and when it grew so tall that it blocked the sun from the farmer's land, the beautiful woman returned to the farmer's cottage with more gifts. There the woman found the farmer and his wife, lying in their garden, under a thick blanket of shade. **Q**

Outside

Charles was looking at the wall when Debbie got out of bed to go to the bathroom. It was three in the morning, but the light was still on, so Charles could see the wall. It was Debbie's wall, her bed, her place.

Charles was looking at the design on the wallpaper. Then he punched the wall as hard as he could.

It sounded to Debbie, in the bathroom, as if something had fallen.

When Debbie came back to bed, Charles was facing the wall, his arm sticking into the wall.

"What happened?" Debbie said.

"I don't know," Charles said. He twisted his head around to look at her. "I went crazy," he said. "The wall's pretty thin."

"Did it hurt?" Debbie said.

"I don't know," Charles said.

His arm was in up to the elbow. He tried to feel if his hand hurt. But he could not feel any pain in it. It just felt cold.

"I think it's outside," he said. "I think I went all the way through."

"Wait a minute," Debbie said. She put some clothes on and went outside. Charles waited. Debbie came back in and said, "It's not out there. I can't see it."

"It feels cold," Charles said. "I'm moving it around. It feels like my arm's outside."

"I couldn't see it," Debbie said, taking off her clothes. She got back into bed with Charles.

Charles wiggled his arm and pulled until it came loose. Some plaster fell on the bed. He sat up and looked in the hole for stars or the moon, but he couldn't see anything. It was black.

"Do you think you'll ever do that again?" Debbie said.

Charles got back under the covers and pressed up against her. Her skin was cold.

It was cold outside.

"I don't think so," Charles said. "Do you?"

"I don't know," Debbie said. "I was just wondering."

"I'll fix it," he said.

"It's okay," she said.

Charles moved his face around in Debbie's hair. It smelled good. He closed his eyes and tried to remember what it was like to be crazy. Then he opened his eyes and looked at his hand. It looked fine. He bent his fingers. They felt fine.

He put his hand on her back.

Debbie turned around to face him. "No, let's go to sleep and do it in the morning," she said.

"Okay," Charles said.

She kissed him, then turned off the light. "Good night, pumpkin," she said.

Charles wondered what he was.

He couldn't sleep. Every time Charles started to drift off, it was no good and he couldn't.

He sat up in bed and looked into the hole again, and this time there was a whole world of stars and moons and planets out there. There were airplanes, too—millions of them, blinking red and white between the stars. It was a world where everyone traveled after midnight. It was a world where everyone traveled and everything was quiet. He wanted her to see it, so he called her name—but she just kept sleeping. Q

The Bullfrog

They came with Shasta daisies in masses, so the flag-stone patio would be more natural in the photographs, they said—and from my color-coordinated early-American bed-room, banished, pouting, crying, dreaming runaway dreams, after being spanked for refusing to clean the blue protozoa-shaped swimming pool, I could hear my father hurl his ginger ale across the kitchen, shouting, *House Beautiful* could god-damn well photograph it the way it was, instead of the way some fag New York photographer thought it ought to look! And next my mother would, of course, come upstairs, mad at me for getting my father upset in the first place, like he really was after that last spanking, since I was about as big as a grownup by this time, which was why I was being banished for not apologizing, for reacting to being ordered to do things in such a tone, as if I was some low slime barely making it across the earth's surface, and just to do his swimming-pool–fancy-house bidding.

And you know what? I was glad he was upset.

Not that cleaning the swimming pool wasn't a job that I even sort of liked—slowly, slowly skimming the leaves and then slowly, even more slowly, sweeping the underwater, black-segmented, tightly wound-up doodlebugs, swirling them just right to swim-dance in whirlpool circles around and around, down and down into the deep blue, into the gently pulling-down drain—seemingly, at least, of their own accord.

From my bedroom picture window I could look across the perfect, rolling St. Augustine grass, where they were bringing the daisies, and bringing the daisies, and arranging the daisies here and there, and my father was out there pacing up and down, showing them at least where to place the goddamn daisies. And I could see all the goings-on out there, just like a movie—the swimming pool embedded in the lawn like a big sparkling jewel in a navel, and my father and all the men hurrying and scurrying back and forth, the sticking-out short sleeves of their summer-white sports shirts stiff little wings, and the photographer and my mother pointing and talking up on the patio, shading their eyes and sometimes patting the heads of the squirming, matching, brindle boxers pushing against their legs, red tongues lolling out of the big, black-as-Tar-Baby, Foo-Dog–grinning mouths.

The truth is that I wanted to be out there, teasing, running with the dogs, or seeing how far to overlean the pool, the skimmer-screen slow-motion-tightrope-one-more-leaf-fencing around and around, until all water surface seemed to vanish into floating sparkles, dazzling the eye that looks now into the mystery-undulating, shadow-blue pool floor, along which I'd then slowly scoot the long-handled brush, firmly feeling along every curving surface, insinuating gradually so as not to stir up the whole pool at once, but persuading, inducing bits of leaves and dirt, a few snails, and hundreds and hundreds of doodlebugs to rise up, whirling and swirling in dozens of undulations from each brushstroke, circle after circle down into the deeper and deeper blue at the inevitable drain at the deepest center at the deepest part of the pool—down there where my sisters and I play mermaids, dancing, transformed underwater to breathless, lithe fish-creatures, never surfacing, but with writhing-seaweed hair—not the rubber caps we really had to wear for keeping the overtreated (our eyes red all summer) pool from being messy, dirty, and disgusting, like some other low somebodies might have things in their pool. But then sometimes we would all three be Esther Williamses, endlessly pursued by Latin men, and only having to hold in our stomachs real hard, take on and off those bathing caps, and back-and-side-stroke up and down the pool a lot, just as in the movies they would take us to see—even before we had to move to this fancy house—on Thursdays, the maid's day off, after having dinner either at the country-club family buffet, or at El

Chico's, for lessons in restaurant manners, and for secret flirt-ings with a particular black-eyed waiter.

But even though I wanted to be out there, saying, "Oh well," and cleaning the pool anyway, how could I give in now to his world's-worst-gloater victory smirks—making it, *So you finally saw it my way,* or else, *And these are all the reasons why I am right,* or even, *I'm acting humble, but I win again and can barely keep a straight face about it.* So I stayed in my room watching the picture-window–daisy-placement–frenzy movie, hearing the *Now, that's what I call music* Big Band sounds piped all over—even outside and even in my room—until I put on my own 45 records and had to keep turning them up louder and louder, until I saw him out there, hearing it and getting that eager-*Aha!*-furious look, wheeling around to charge the house and then my room, yelling about trashy nigger music—music like would be played by the kind of kids that would have the nerve to drive up in a carful to my father's fancy house, yelling, "Hey, let's go swimming!" But I knew that if I did that, he might just go crazy again, the way I had seen and heard him go crazy before—with drinking and breaking things, and going out with guns in the night, and then even being forced and tied and carried away with a crash and a cry that I can't forget, and with her saying, "What are you doing up?"—as if something was my fault. And then him coming back after months, and being bathrobe-sad in the house for more months. So I was really a chicken about if those kids were my friends, and if they drank beer and got hair or grass in the pool—so it was hopeless, maybe—and they might be, like he said, just taking advantage of my having a swimming pool, and then, *How could I be friends with those people?* and, *How could I listen to what wasn't even music?* and, *If I didn't change my tune, I would find myself on my own out on the street someday.*

So then my mother would come in again for a talking-to about why couldn't I just humor him instead of just-like-him always having to stir up some kind of big upset. "Why can't we just be happy?" she would say, looking at me—me glaring at the floor and hiding under my pillow my secret paperback about the bulging-yellow-sweater-named-Tomboy girl, who always gets in trouble with the tying-people-up threatening-them-with-cigarette-burns leader of the gang, who is secretly her boyfriend, but neither one of them knows it. I wouldn't say much, and she would say that maybe I could think about it while they were out for the evening. But I knew I wouldn't think about it, but would wait until they were gone to their dinner party at some other ready-to-be-photographed-for-*House-Beautiful*-type house, me babysitting and waiting until dark outside—and all the Shasta daisies white ghosts of flowers in the dark—to go out and turn on the pool light, to there find a giant spotted-golden bullfrog come up from the creek where he used to swim flat out for miles, but now he was trapped in the glowing, undulating, bluer-than-blue pool, powerful legs pumping and stretching to coast the blue width and length—pushing off from one side and then the other, from one end and then the other, stirring the whole pool and all the leaves and doodlebugs into whirlpools on all sides of his repeated, frantic, trapped path, back and forth and up and down, with no place to get a leg up, banging back and forth— that bullfrog, leapfrog, frog-in-the-throat—pushing off the deep, then the shallow, then the deep, then the shallow, ranging the shape and size of the pool, being the shape and size of the pool, forgetting that there was ever anything else but the shape and size of the pool. **Q**

ANN PYNE

In the Form of a Person

We were hunting for wilderness, my mother-in-law up
ahead, the four of us sisters-in-law behind. Mount Robson was
up there too—still farther up there—distant as a postcard,
snow-covered. There were gift shops, yes. Off to the side of us
they kept showing themselves, coyote-like, unsetting our children. The golf course claimed the men, at least four of them,
as well as my mother-in-law, and therefore me. My youngest
brother-in-law only carried his intention differently—clipped
it up in a fortified guitar case.

We had come a long way. The flying had been three-
stopped, fraught with colored pencils wedged into the cre-
vasses of seat cushions, falling through with our attempts,
scrape-knuckled, to save them, all of us loading and unloading
the mule pack of our shoulders. My mother-in-law was in what
she called her good-luck traveling outfit—an Ultrasuede pants
suit with the Ultrasuede fibers rubbed from the seat of it,
from under the arms of it, from the belly of it, from one
side of it—her good-luck purse like a shotgun rubbing there,
I suppose.

We met the others in Vancouver, a city on the farthest
edge west, built to be started out from: a ridge of sailboats, a
ridge of vehicles, a ridge of sharp rock face half-naveling up
around it. There we had bought the talisman of beavers, owls,
bears that the children had insisted on, the outpost of contra-
band cigars. There, too, we had argued—should we detour to
Polynesia to eat or eat right there in the lobby salad bar? It was
a hairline fracture none of us drew attention to, our shin that
it appeared on—Polynesia had cost too much, the children-in-
laws had not liked egg roll.

From the Canadian Pacific Railway Station we took the
train. The girls were swimming under the "Great White" cow-

boy hat my father-in-law had collected from Australia, the tops of their faces bitten off. There was a blue-outfitted, epauletted ticket seller who was to reappear later as our conductor, which was slightly disconcerting—as if the ruse of the thing had been exposed after there was no time left to pull out. He was organizing the bags for our two-day journey up there to the Rockies, checking our tickets off under a gold-featured, gold-rimmed clock, big as the moon is. Off on the dim borders of the place, the children had accosted one of us, and then the others of us—they had wanted this, they had wanted that. For a short while it was as it might have been in heaven—each of us coming in from behind in defense of one another; then the first of us gave in, and then the next—it was the Alamo. Still there in the station, we were lined up like organ pipes for the photograph of the group of us. The marble floors there had been clean enough to roll around on, bullet-wounded.

"Jouez mal, mais jouez vite," my mother-in-law says.

It is one of her "I have personality" lines for a little light humor around the camp fire. "For God's sake, don't play bridge, then," will heel-yap us next, meant, as it usually is, for my father-in-law. "He reads the most complicated, most theoretical bridge books, and then he does this," she says—by which she means, "He cannot digest bear meat anymore, you know; he will have to be left on the trail soon; a few sticks to make a fire with."

At me, my mother-in-law is exasperated. This time in front of everyone I have one-upped her on how to play bridge without a bridge table. Her plan was worked out whereby the thinnest of us is made to push over so that the cards can be played there on the seat. The dummy she will arrange on a piece of cardboard pegged up between the extra-ness of her hip and the window ledge. I, on the contrary, have unscrewed, with the help of the conductor and her richest son, the Plexiglass that protects a TRAVEL CANADA poster. This we balance between us—no insult to anyone—on the butt end of the cardboard box the train lunches came to us packed in.

Jasper. The name is evocative. Put your finger on exotica and go there to the green-eyed lake, it seemed to say, still does. But when we put our feet down on the ground there, we see people in the soft shoes of old people, dressed in dresses of the city and blazers made of madras.

We are taken to our rooms, led up and down the mini-sidewalked hills, the cabins arranged on either side of us like tour-bus seats. The cabin we will sleep in is one of the big old ones at the far end of the place. Through the pines we see the fleshy color of its logs flickering the way the flank of a big deer would flicker.

In 1901, the Queen Mother slept there.

We are eager to get there first, get the room nearest my mother- and father-in-law so that they can hear the yip and howl of us in love. My first brother-in-law and his wife are a Fax machine and a car-pool leader from the suburbs; we can outdo all of them.

I am despondent. The garbage cans here sunk into so much concrete it seems it is the garbage that is threatening, not the grizzlies. The stone urn, or whatever shape it is that this adventure might have held for us, split up already into too much tourist paraphernalia to keep track of. Even the trophy of one's children to be shared on the mantlepiece of three other aunts and uncles, if indeed the trophy could be won. Then there is this: My mother- and father-in-law have held preference out from us—set themselves in a separate cabin, equidistant to what commotion any of us might have tried for.

That first night we ate together, had to. "More mother's milk, please," my mother-in-law says, pushing her glass toward the champagne bottle as if she were deploying troops. "Mack the Knife" was playing—my brother-in-law, the richest one I told you of, had requested it to catch his parents both off guard thirty years back under the moon somewhere. But my mother-in-law devours up his intention—"How darling of you"—and spits it out like drink she sniffs the poison in; no favor can be curried.

By day, first day out, we find how the land lies. Rowboats, paddleboats, canoes, Windsurfers to move around the emerald lake in. Ping-Pong, pool, pool pool, slot machines, for which the children are constantly draining us. There are gift shops in the lobby, gifts shops where you rent the boats from, gift shops that come through housekeeping. We sign for trips. Tuesday, the Athabasca Glacier, Thursday, Maligne Lake. Here's what we learn: the mountains, as mountains are everywhere, are people-named. This particular place, the area between Medicine Lake and Maligne Lake, since it could be passed around, was left late for exploring, finally broken through to by a woman. Medicine Lake, the first of the lakes we get to, empties itself annually, leaves its green mischief in a pool somewhere far down from here. Maligne Lake, Lake of Evil, gets its name from the dangers of the white-water river— viewable on video—flowing from it. We take a slow cruise boat way far out on Maligne Lake to a little island where everyone poses, glaciers in the distance. My daughter—she's a fool— shoots up all three cartridges of film she has on the backs of people we don't know the names of. "We don't want them," I'll have to say to her later at the gates of our scrapbook, losing thereby those territories of moral generousness a mother does not like to have to move back from. Back in our closed-in boat, the bunch of us are rowdy, swing the boat's doors in and out, threaten like outlaws. Those who are respectable whisper among themselves, exude the unenforcability of sigh-laws.

My mother- and father-in-law have distanced themselves five or six rows in front of us—we would have to flock-shoot to get at them now; will have to wait for later on up the trail for the "gramma" call to knee-whack them back a bit.

We have been gone almost days now, this pencil dragging its slight spoor of roughness across paper. The children are away from here, slurring down the Athabasca River in a great barge of a raft, I escaping its watery imposition up my socks, my sleeves; escaping my child in a wet-lap cuddle; the hairline fracture that we got over Polynesia beginning to ache, opening wider, especially for my staying here, drier than the others. The parents-in-law are ahead of us on the golf course, practicing for what we must join them at tomorrow. Sometimes by the roadside, yes, we have seen some wilderness. You can always tell how much by the parked-car buildup on the shoulders, as for an accident.

Coming back from the Athabasca Glacier was something pretty big. It was drizzly. I was in the back, from where you had to push the seat up to stumble out. My child was just succeeding admirably at insulting the clear-voiced talent of her ancestor by singing "Found a Peanut" loudly in her ancestor's ear—my mother-in-law's. Damn this trip, I say to myself, so worth-it-full you can never turn your back, not on anything.

The horns were magnificent.

The moose carried them hypnotized above him, a body's worth in span.

How easy, in the haze of this, to forget what we have come here for; to subsist on half victories—picking up puzzle pieces, sorting clothes, bagging them for the main lodge's dry cleaning service, that occasional roadside bit of wilderness I just told you of, twice around the lake on mountain bikes. My son makes it on his own once, the tail of his Davy Crockett cap rising in the wind behind him. Up and down the little knee-high hills, the gnarled, unexpected ones the toe bones of tree roots put up wobbling you out over a bobby-pin bend of turn overlooking the sharp green water rocks beneath your front wheel. We stopped at a little peninsula along the path where there was a bench put down for pilgrims such as us. I knew that tomorrow my son would walk his bike around this same trail, stiffen his legs like oars, dry-paddling the ground on either side of him, afraid again to ride. We said a prayer on that bench, looking out at what my mother-in-law keeps referring to as Mount Edith Clavell—my son's, a prayer of thanks for the glory of taking the trail the way he just has; mine, that he would never—not in some siege of grief, not in some faraway war— have to stretch his abilities as far above himself again as this.

I am getting soft.

Today, as predicted, the miracle of my son on his bike has tempered nothing, is sustenance for some campfire far from here but not for here. Today he sat with his tow-headed cousin on the steps of the hot tub, old men already, hunched like eagles.

Mount Edith Clavell is what they keep talking of. Everyone does. Of an excursion to its base. What for? I keep asking. The Athabasca Glacier, which is the grander glacier, has already been found by us, snow-dirty as the Madison Avenue bus discharging itself. We have skied the glaciers up near heaven, my husband and I have.

"It looks like Dad," my third brother-in-law says, and the others agree, all looking up ceremoniously to where Mount Edith Clavell stretches her juts and jagged edges along the horizon. Indeed, without stretching the imagination too far, you can see the long, lazy rise of the stomach, the up and down of a snore when the clouds cover and uncover it, the chin of a mountain, the nose of a mountain, the forehead of a mountain. At dinner my second brother-in-law tells me, wincing down a sip of his vodka gimlet, "In a year or two he will be up there like that, you know," he says. "Mother is ten years younger, you know," he goes on, wincing again.

Last night it snowed up there. The snow was spread across his chin, across his nose, my second brother-in-law confides to me. By the fifth hole of noon, it was no longer like a bandanna, had warmed off to well beneath the nose but no farther—the snow he cannot brush from himself, the white grizzle of his no longer shaving.

My father-in-law is waning.

You can see it in the way his feet move when he is up there dancing—small pockets of breath only between each step. His golf swing shows it, too. At the moment of contact, he slows it, almost stops it. The ball is not egg-soft, we almost start to tell him, as if an age-befitting kindness for all things living was what had him in its grasp, unfitting him for what we have to do here. He is gentle with the children. Lets them talk. Lets them throw stones.

The children have trail names now—Bouceronymous, Bealeyophagus, opaque as everything else seems. My sisters-in-law have broken into character traits—civilness, organization, stockings at night, the thank-you note. With everyone watching, I can take no shot at the flying-down-wind covey they now compose themselves of, the low craft of them settling. My mother-in-law is the only pay dirt left; I know her ways like bear tracks.

I have got her to myself, canoeing out in Lake Beauvert, close to the middle of it. My son and her grandson, one and the same, sits low, almost invisible, between us. We talk across him the way lovers would their beard. I have forced him out of the way with three persons, one person always is forced out.

She is a strong rower, I am too. Neither she nor I knows the slippery twist of the "J." A bond that is part muscle, part non-finickiness, part not the middle-classness of Camp Manodnock, that is my sisters-in-law. What it comes down to is this: Who can do the most things? I can play golf, tennis, bridge, talk about politics. She can, too, my mother-in-law. But none of them can. I also have a straight-up-the-fall-line way of getting to know people, can strike up an intimacy faster with the friends of my mother-in-law than an old pro can strike a fire up. It relaxes them, lets their shoulders down, lets the sap of talk run through the tree of them. Whereas what my sister-in-laws do—one of them, at least two of them—is hold the flint too tight, watch for the spark with too much concentration.

My latest sister-in-law, the third one, and my youngest brother-in-law, they know the yip and howl I was speaking of earlier, I have found that out. As well they seek the heart of our mother-in-law, seek to please, to ingratiate themselves.

But I dissect my difficulties, render my own children up, draw my mother-in-law toward me as one draws in any old predator, pretending sickness in the group.

My youngest sister and brother-in-law will not go the distance.

You will see.

Look, for instance, at my sister-in-law now. She and my brother-in-law, with my conjoining too—which will set me back a bit, I know—have composed a song for the grandchildren to sing. There have been hours and hours of trapping the right rhymes, singing around the lake on our bicycles. It is aimed not just at the heart of my mother-in-law but at my father-in-law's heart, too. My sister-in-law is there now singing it—she is Julie Andrews; my brother-in-law, guitar across his leg—he is the Baron von Trapp. The children are up there too, falling off from either side of my brother and sister-in-law, the bunch of them this time passing themselves off like a springtime slope-of-meadow.

Now watch my mother-in-law in the face of it.

She pretends fidgeting with her camera. She shifts to photograph the audience. She keeps the camera tight as goggles to her eyes, protecting against anything that might come from this, sends a message to my father-in-law, loud enough for the farthest back along the trail of us to hear—she wants that certain wine at dinner; the children's chickie right with our first course.

She has eluded us again, the heart of her has. I could have told you.

There are ways to get her yet.

On the putting green, for instance, the white of golf shoes moving just a little at the corner of her vision unnerves my mother-in-law. The trick, therefore—to position oneself a little beyond where such a movement ought justifiably to be bothersome, but still in sight. Or better yet, I can annoy her with the red herring of my anxiety—a little fish bait on the trail in front of the large cat of her, a ruse with which the elements are seeming to cooperate, sending now a wind and a darkly clouding sky coming toward us.

The gun of my tongue starts off light in my mouth.

The sun is still out, there is a breeze, as yet just a brisk one. It's a one-more-club-than-usual day, I know that. But when my mother-in-law says, "Take one more club than usual," I say, when she thinks she has just told me what we should do about the wind, "No, I mean what shall we do about the wind?"

This baffles her, of course. It's a brain whiff just before she goes to hit the ball. Then when she says "What?" taking a nibble up, I wait until she has started back across the fairway to make her shot before I say, "I mean not about the wind here, I mean about the wind there."

The mountain called Mount Home was up in front of us. It was a dark shard of earthenware left stood-on-end, an old piece of pot too far from the temple of my mother-in-law's golf for her to care about. Mount Home was where the children were, on a tram going straight up its face line.

From where we are, no sinew of metal cable can be seen coming from the pellet of the tram; it is a little egg making its way down the fluidy air, nothing holding it there—although of course, there is. "It's what's up there I am worried about," I almost yell to my mother-in-law across the fairway after she has missed her shot, which is part of what I mean, rendering my children up. "It's about the children up *there.*"

Now a wind really was up. It was the kind of wind that has slaps in it; the kind of wind that funnels sand right from sand traps. It was breaking old-lady-small tree limbs all over the place. From the opposite direction of where Mount Home was, a primordial swirl of blackness appeared. "Do you think they'll shut it down?" I yell to my husband.

"Damn it!" my husband yells, "I've always hated those damned cable cars!"—his voice its usual scaring-off-the-prey loudness.

Our words are acting out the nightmare of bad golfers, which none of us are—shanking, slicing, hooking, dribbling off toward each other.

I insist on quitting.

My mother-in-law insists on going on.

"You can't do anything about it, anyway," she says.

She has eleven of them up there. Three sons, three daughters-in-law, and five grandchildren.

I had started out joking, I will grant you that. Now my heart is hanging out from my body. Anyone could take it like a coat off a hook if they knew it was out there.

"Your sister-in-law would never," she starts in. "Your brother-in-law would never," she starts in again, holds her hand on her golf hat, removes her hand, tries to putt before the wind takes the hat off—that's all she's thinking of. She says this same thing about the other sisters-in-law, the other brothers-in-law. She says it again, to keep me playing on. The fairway between us has turned leaf-strewn, old. If it were not for the book my daughter held in her hand, the first one she has read on her own ever, and the Davy Crockett cap my son set off with to keep himself brave in, I could have almost let go of them.

I am strong, you know. If you have ever seen those televised nature shows, you have seen me walk down trees. And you have seen this, too—seen me bend my slow knees to the huddle of my young that cannot go on farther. "Come on, come on, you must leave them now," you are begging me. But I am thick-headed, also, as an elephant. My knees stay bent even though she is trying to get me up again.

She tries to nudge me up, then whip me up, pitting me against one sister-in-law, then again against the other.

I am doing all this about elephants in a country where there are no elephants, which must enrage her, I know that. I toss aside what she cares about like entrails not from bear or elk or moose but a buzzard. I refuse to begin over on the putting green of a new life.

She tries one taunt further.

I curse her.

Never mind the word I used. The word is either oversized as a pair of fourteen-point antlers back in a one-bedroom, 11-J apartment, or puny as a pair of horns a taxidermist should not have wasted time on. Suffice it to say, it was a trail-like epithet not suitable for the mowed fairway of the hole we were on.

She was an absolute wilderness, my mother-in-law. She was the Law of Life you leave the sick behind on, keep your heart light with.

I yelled it at her, my curse going low as an un-teed-up two iron goes straight for the target. She stepped aside, left it harmless as moose turd she saw before stepping. It was I who had stepped wrong, snapped a twig at what I had been so long on the track of.

I watch the mountain called Mount Home while we finish playing, at least while they finish playing. The tram went up. It came back down. It went up again. The wind had gone calm. The sun came out, friendly as pinto patches. A shard of earthenware still up there standing on end, the sky still sublimely ochred behind it, Mount Home was no longer where the children were. I feel, for more holes than I can bear, the heaviness of my mother-in-law pushing down on me. She is all glacier— rocks, stones, twigs to preserve the icy heart of her. Against my will, the weight of her pushes me toward the warming in the valley. I apologize.

She drains the blood from her face the way mothers empty pleasure from a bathtub.

I wheedle, I cajole, do all else I can.

I can undo none of it, can make nothing more pass across the stoniness of her features.

As could be predicted, or, if you get down on hands and knees on the too-thick carpet they have in the cabin's living room, you can see my mother-in-law's tracks over to the couch where she has laid herself down, the wound internal, high as her chest is.

This is a camouflage, I know. The heart pain, the graying into history, the let-muscle-loose into layer on layer of skin lapped into a weighted flatness. If you will draw around closer, I will tell you how I know this: My real mother turned manatee on me once, my father and I trying to slap her back with the fast, unallowed rudder movements of our too-blunt hands. But we couldn't get down deep enough to get where she had gone to. I tried to take back something I had said to her; my father called for the ambulance.

When I say camouflage, I mean that when the ambulance came, my mother sat straight up out of hers, the mini-win of my retraction hidden now somewhere in the folds of her night-gown where she knew neither of us would have the stomach to go looking for it, my father had not in years.

Now it was my mother-in-law doing this—blooded as she could get, stretched out flat. But my mother-in-law was not as wiley as my real mother, would not slip out cold the way my real mother had. I stayed on the edge of the room, the fret region I was so much practiced in.

We go to dinner. I at dinner trying to pass what happened off like bad air. My mother-in-law at dinner passing nothing to no one. Stoney-faced still, it seems the makeup she has chosen was made for the occasion—all in tones of rocks, of molds. At night I dream, sleep fitfully. There is nothing to be seen out the small high window of the bathroom of the long dark mountain sleeping up there in the form of a person. I try to do something with the hard knot of what is in my stomach. I lie back in the bed, my heart thumping. I have served her my children and she has eaten them. I have her slippery heart in my pocket like a golf ball. A sense of pity, as for an animal leg-trapped in a trap, comes in over me.

The next morning, early, the big-headed moose all the way up nibbling at the red geraniums in our window box is the first sign of our victory.

We go riding.

A different trip this time, there are bear, real coyote, deep ravines, angry welts of rivers cutting through stone. My sister-in-law, my youngest one, stops her horse, dismounts, leads him off the trail. The sound of our own importance loud in our ears, I accept the great force of urine I hear as belonging to her. It is my brother-in-law, the youngest and the humblest of us, who reminds us of the delicacy we have been commissioned for: that it is not she but the immense barrel of her horse letting loose, pumping its barrage down into the ground.

All the while that we were riding, I had in sight the mountain that my brothers-in-law call Edith Clavell, that they see in the form of their father. But the mountain had not the chin the father did, the nose the father did, the forehead the father did, and yet they went on dreaming the mountain in this form—it is amazing—when it is the chin the mother has, the nose the mother has, the forehead the mother has, when it is the mother herself up there beyond where the wolves go, cast up there by me, or so today it seems to me—the me, mind you, the one she likes; the me, mind you, who arranges her how she likes to be arranged—up there, faced up there into the sky, so that she need not see, nighttimes, and daytimes too, for that matter, what she will not look at—the spectacle of us, me and her first born, the two of us, hind to fore, at it—yes—fucking.

Today, tonight, there is meat for everyone. For all the children, there are books. For my daughter, a little glass-faceted bear, its belly the size of a pinky fingernail. And ice cream, too—pistachio almond fudge. There is no end of it, the spoils. No end to coming back to what is civilized.

I know, I know. Victory is the tall-tale country to those who have not been out there, I know that—the scene of a little stone throw in a puddle that turns, with just the telling of it, into the dilation of a lake-size orgasm. It happens one, two, three times without my husband's having to throw more stones in.

But listen to this; this you can believe:

At dinner I dance with my father-in-law; he has requested of me that I do so.

We start off slow.

I have to lead him in his steps, so great is the frailness of his intention. Now I am making his steps come out of him without his even trying. "Something fast," he says, "with a little more pep. How about the 'A Train,' do you know that one?" my father-in-law asks the piano player, my father-in-law pretending not to know—he's the cooney one, still the chief—that the music comes from the tape deck at the piano player's side, that there is nothing the piano player knows or does not know, nothing that comes from the damp and fast wilderness of fingertips on slats of ivory blade the way it used to.

This wins my husband's heart—his father and me up there dancing. I can tell you how pleased my husband is, he always is. It is as if he is me up there chosen by his father for dancing while the three of his brothers are made to sit and watch.

He forgives me everything.

My husband always does.

You see, his heart was my first kill, the cinchiest. **Q**

Born on the Fourth of July

So you think you know everything.

About life, crime, tropical disease, Chinese resorts, Braille, sex, Siamese analysts, levitation, Amelia Earhart, Cedar Key, Billy Budd, Wallis Simpson, the Straits of Magellan, wedding rings, gin rummy, Johnnie Walker, supper clubs in northern Wisconsin.

Erase.

Now what we have here is a pink stone.

Knowing nothing.

Resting on white sand.

A light breeze.

A flat round pink warm stone. Lying with other stones on a white-sand beach. The breeze comes off the sea, the leaves of the sea grape move. There are no other sounds. Wind, leaf, water, sand. The stone neither wants, nor wants not.

So, like, she said, leaning there against the door. Like, hi! I'm taking a survey? She was wearing her pollster's uniform. A blue leather jacket, a small blue gun on a leather cord, black evening dress with jet beads, pointed shoes, stars on her ears, fried calamari hair. A woman after my own taste, I who wear next to nothing, so anxious to avoid the raffish costume of the teenager, the look of the aging rock star.

So, like, do you travel? Lovers? Do you have a good attitude? No. Practice prenatal care? What do you want out of life? I want to acquire. Once so interested in others, I now want more. Only more. More. The word makes my mouth water.

Also, like, what toothpaste? I might want to see your medicine cabinet. Tabulate your shelf life.

Forget it. That cabinet looks like the office of a poor dentist trying to build a practice deep in Tennessee. His name is what? Louise. Midge. *Are* there women dentists? And where's to travel? The Mayan ruins? Reindeer country? Florida. That brown dreamland sticking down toward the tropics, displaying playful oranges and an American gloom that seems to have coated the fairways and the coast roads, sealing them with a kind of deadly nail polish, stopping the waters that feed the fountain of youth. China? Very dusty, my mother writes from Peking. Yes, I'm sorry to say, P. Peking.

Prenatal care?

Oh baby.

Back then you smoked Chesterfields. You drank martinis. You ate blue meat. Run over the coals. Not even warm. It is awful to remember. You wore alligator shoes and carried alligator bags, painted green, and hair spray and a hat with a veil that stuck to your lipstick smile. You had children. They grew up. You did not worry about how to give to them. You worried about them inhaling what was left to you. You shouted, Let me out, let me out. There was no reply. Today people talk about health. Exercise. Diet. Water. Drink a lot of water. Forget eggs. Hold the mayo. Run. Run up and down. Don't have ether. Have the baby. Feed it. Love it so much. Look it in the eye. Say, You are here. We are here. Cheers.

I have friends who played Mozart on a cassette next to their baby's cradle, in the cradle, in the baby, in the baby's perfect well-loved ear, all night long, the world's tiniest orchestra whispering yadadaa, yadadee, and the baby's memory already remembering, already gathering in the sounds, gently, sweetly pressing them in before it was too late and its ears were stuffed up with ink, and birds' nests, and candles, and peacock feathers, and no pitch, no pitch pipe, no memory of song, *nada*, nothing. A tonette wailing "Bye Bye Blackbird." Bye-bye.

I have friends two years later, same friends, who fed their child pasta, pasta pesto, pasta primavera for the birthday, then duck, and duck liver, and duck breasts, and duck salad, and Peking duck; who took the child to Peking, who held it between them and said, There now, there there, the Great Wall, the Peking Wall, the Beijing Wall, the Peijing—Jeiping—whatever wall, but your wall, darling, from us to you. The East. A world *we* will never see because now it is too late and no more tourists are allowed inside. The pockets are full. All hands are squeezed and we are left with these blotty postcards and bottles with Yangtze River water drying in them. A stuffed duck. A battery-operated silkworm.

My children stayed home and ate white things. Terrible things. Cool Whip, Marshmallow Fluff, mushroom soup, tuna fish, fish fingers, pillows. Calm, albino food. Moby Dick dinners, we called them.

Anything burned gives color, the pollster said. Not to mention shaved carrots. She lay on the window seat dragging negatives up from the negative box, holding them to the light, squinting. Like, these are your children? Why don't they have more hair? This is the guy? Look at him. He got fat! Wearing a plaid suit. Like some plaid mattress! Why do all of you look like subtitle types? Did you go to a war?

We had a child once—blue balls. Small *b*, l-u-e, small *b*, a-l-l-s. Someone puckering for life, someone innocent who was abandoned. The size of capers, but even they were blue. A three-pound miracle born on the Fourth of July. When the ice cream had melted into the grass, and Niagara Falls and the Statue of Liberty had sizzled out over the lake, and the Drum and Bugle Corps had marched up Main Street, as they had when we were children, up at the top of the house on summer nights, fluttering like little moths against the light, then he was born. He hardly lived.

He was gone, and I don't know what became of him. We did not talk about him. For dinner that Saturday we went to the house I had grown up in. We had baby carrots, baby beets, baby zucchini, baby potatoes, baby cauliflower, baby rolls— had the kitchen gone mad—and red, white, and blue hollandaise, and fillet of beef, each neatly sliced blood-red dead slice oozing cool bloody juice across the thick porcelain plates from France, at the dining-room table from England, beside screens from China, where nightingales sang on burnt-orange branches, looking out toward the Japanese trees bending over the lake that went nowhere, our inland sea slowly filling up with salt from the Atlantic, and over it all, the Midwestern silence, emptiness, stillness, the stillness of a breeze drifting over flat land, and alewives burning on the shore.

I could use nail polish, the pollster said. Something dark? She replaced the stars on her ears with fake fur bats and thumbed through the *Denver Restaurant Guide.* The person I admire, she said, is the Duchess of Windsor. She was married to a king. Her sheets were ironed.

After the dinner, my husband's uncle, just in from Santa Fe, hardly the world's quickest, said, When is it coming? Aren't you . . . uh. Two years in the desert had given him a look. Chunks of adobe and pieces of Indian blanket stuck in the hair. Shreds of Georgia O'Keeffe's torn black bathrobe for a necktie. No eyelid muscles, just a spare turquoise finger propping the lid open. He shrugged, puffed on a Haitian Comme il Faut that touched my bare shoulder, burning and blistering the skin, and smiled that sunning lizard's smile. Would you be interested in fucking? Well?

Twenty-five years after that night, I ran into him again at a Cuban country club in Miami. He was submerged to his armpits in a cigar-shaped pool, playing gin rummy at a floating bar, drinking a kiwi daiquiri. Last night I was introduced to the President of a secret country, he reported. By wire. We were having dinner, a very small party, a very special party. And a call came through. I was among Internationals. We were all in white. I was invited to step to the phone, to say. He paused and grinned. Unbelievable, I cried. And he said what? Hello, presumably.

The pollster put on leather gloves and began to cut out the fingertips. The rule at funerals, she said, is only immediate family is supposed to be in the first car. Husbands and wives don't go together. The deceased should wear lipstick. You're not allowed to tamper with your own mailbox.

After I'd auctioned off the wedding ring, I took my best

friend to Harry's Bar for lunch. The place was dripping with long yellow and white furs, with big sleeves and heads of animals caught up in their own bad dreams. Fur fur, I thought, we'll choke on the fur. On a hair ball. There is going to be fur in the chicken, in the wine, in the lemon mousse. Big wads.

My friend said she wanted a glass of water, then a very dry martini with an olive. And a man! She laughed. And then she said, Oh, my God. Because there he was. In the glass, just sloshing about in the gin, a small, good-looking man in a yellow silk-shantung suit, and a pale pink shirt, and black patent-leather dancing pumps, and a raincoat, and a black Dunhill cigarette holder and cool shades. He was floating on his back, waving and calling out. Excuse me. Hello. Der hash been un collashul mishundershtanding. We bent over the glass. His voice was so new and cramped. He had opened his eyes that morning to find himself with earlobes and a plum-colored tongue, a gold filling, and ten toes and two legs. But it was not a happy arrangement for someone at home in urban kitchens, in Eastern European hallways. To wake to find one-self in a new country, in another age, made man, with pushy parents and bad health.

My friend plucked the little fellow from the gin and wrapped him gently in a napkin and propped him against the salt shaker. When we looked again, he had been cleared away.

In a napkin, the pollster said. The guy I'm with has a convertible. You should see his hair blow! People have to have their lives. For now, I need a shot of you. She took the gun off the neck cord and pulled the trigger and a light popped.

Cute. Still, I jumped and raised my hand to cover the tear I felt in my arm, while she counted nine and peeled off a black square that gave birth to a picture of someone with the far-off gaze of a golf pro or a sea captain.

Do you believe in love? the pollster asked. Do you care for boudoir sets? She was already putting things into paper bags. The silver oyster forks, and the negatives, and the white li-queur with the coffee beans floating around. The new vacuum cleaner, the annual report from the Mayo Clinic, the wedding pictures. The living children's baby clothes packed in neat white cardboard boxes and tied with ribbon. The money frozen into the ice cubes. The silent butler. You'll never use that, I told her. Or the bonbon dishes. But they were into silver, she said. They were setting up in Sarasota. He jumped his convertible through fire there. She had her vanishing act. They wanted everything. Because, she said, you never can tell. She tipped her chin. It was a form of goodbye.

Never let go of the people you love. Tighten the rope, soak the fiber, right? Because people slip away. All people become the slipping-down man. Fading there in your cupped hand. On motorcycles spinning across the desert floor, on corks, waterborne on whatever sea, on telephone wires twanging in a northern wind. They fold their fingers in childlike cathedrals, until those same fingers stiffen and dawn breaks on the steeples of the dead. They forget. When you call they say, Who? Speak up. I have no daughter living in La Paz. One by one, they burn their houses down and send the furniture to auction. And the ashes of the loved one are dropped over the Pacific, same-day service, five hundred down, and you keep the mink stole.

So of course I buzzed off, too. A bloody mess and butter knives sticking out of my ears, but traveling light all the same. A string bag, a pack of cards, a lime. Wind, leaf, water, song, I sang. Shooting down Highway 9, tangled hair streaming through open windows, through frames where windows had been, through rings of fire, through smoke and smoke rings, trailing dollar bills on kite strings, spinning a Brody toward the sun. Hands on the wheel of misfortune, tough as farmhands, planting hands, plow legs and plow hands, with a salt timer marking the hours and the Southern Cross and the Great Bear marking the days, and a lifeline taking a last high-flying palm leap before the heart settled down, and the skin turned from a rich monkey brown to the memorable sweet soft yellow of a ripe banana, and the bones made folds as soft and as empty as old flannel pockets, but the eyes were still as blue as the Gulf, just shot through with the thin red lines of a cartographer gone a little mad, with the waving marks of the world's great railroads, or the mule paths that led up from Acapulco and over the Sierras to Vera Cruz, in the days of the China trade, when the Manila galleons brought pearls and silks and cinnamon and pepper and fruit-eating bats that tasted like chicken, in the time of explorers and buccaneers. **Q**

Moving In

My father was a big man, over six feet, and I had not known him very well. I was explaining this to George Brunner, my landlord, who lived upstairs and had come down for a talk. We were drinking beer, or he was. I had just moved into the efficiency and didn't trust him. I held the neck of a bottle as I talked, but I did not really drink any.

"You didn't know him very well?" George Brunner said. "What, did he skip town on you when you were little, or what? If you don't mind me asking."

"He died when I was sixteen," I said. I looked toward the kitchenette, where there were some boxes piled. I supposed that tomorrow I'd get to unpacking them. "He lived with us till I was sixteen, but I didn't know him very well. He worked nights," I said.

"He worked nights?" George Brunner said.

"Yes," I said. I looked up at the light fixture. It was bare. I wondered whose responsibility it was to provide a cover for it, the landlord's or mine. Where did one get such a thing? I was about to ask him, but he leaned forward in his chair.

"What kind of job he have, working at night?" The landlord pulled a fresh beer out of the pack on the floor and yanked the cap off with his teeth. This was his fourth beer, and I was surprised that he hadn't gotten up to use the bathroom yet. He seemed to be thinking hard about something.

"He was a proofreader," I said. "For a law firm."

"Those places work at night?" the landlord said, staring at me. "Every night?"

"He left the house at four and got home past one in the morning," I said.

"New York's a funny place, huh? Lawyers working all night." The landlord swallowed some beer. "Lawyers work all night, or they stop at one?"

"My father wasn't a lawyer," I said. "He just worked for them." I was still thinking about the fixture.

George Brunner said, "You say you didn't know him?"

"Not very well," I said.

The man put his beer down on the arm of my mother's old easy chair. I would have gotten up to find him a coaster, but I did not want to seem rude.

"You live in New York all your life?" George Brunner said.

"Until last year," I said.

"Hah," he said. "You told me that." He picked up his beer as if about to drink, then put it down and held it there, on the arm of the chair. "What'd you leave New York for?"

"Too crowded," I said.

"I can see what you mean," the landlord said. "I was to New York once."

I nodded. I was rolling the bottle between my hands. I looked at the clock above the stove. It was time for the landlord to be leaving. I began to lift myself off the sofa bed.

The man settled himself more deeply into my mother's old chair. "I like to know my tenants," he said.

"That's always a good idea," I said.

The landlord said, "When you know your tenants, they don't skip out on you." He gave me a significant look.

"I imagine not," I said, drumming my fingers against the beer. "I hope I don't look like the type who'd skip town."

"No," he said. "Girls usually don't. Women, I mean."

"But it's good to be safe," I said.

"That's what I always say," the landlord said. He tilted his bottle to his mouth, emptied it, and burped. The six-pack on the floor had one bottle left in it. "You'll probably want that one for yourself, for later," the landlord said.

"No," I said. "I really don't drink very much. Go ahead." I propped my bottle between my knees and bent to pass him the one from the pack. "Here," I said. "Help yourself."

"I really shouldn't."

"Go on," I said.

He wrenched off the cap with his teeth again. With teeth that strong, he couldn't be that old, I thought.

George Brunner said, "How'd your daddy die, if you don't mind me asking?"

"Mugged," I said.

"Mugged?" The landlord repeated the word as though it were foreign to him.

"Mugged is when you get robbed," I said.

George Brunner was offended. "I know what 'mugged' is," he said. "But how'd he die of it?"

I shrugged and blinked. The light was hurting my eyes. It had been a long night and I was tired. "They wanted his money and he didn't have enough of it, I guess. It was when he was coming home from work. At the train station. Near home. There were three of them."

The landlord whistled through his teeth. "They killed him? Murdered him?"

I thought a moment. They were not words I would have used. Then I nodded.

"Why, that's horrible," the landlord said.

I said I guessed it was. We were both quiet for a while. Everything was quiet. Then the bottle slipped from between my knees and emptied out onto my lap and the carpet before I could right it. The landlord jumped up from his chair.

"Do you have paper towels or anything?" George Brunner said. "Anything at all?"

I looked toward the kitchenette. The metal towel holder was empty, its flaps inverted. The boxes, unopened, stood closed in their stacks by the sink. I supposed there must be dish towels in there somewhere, but when I thought about hunting through the cartons with the landlord looking on, I decided to forget it. I rubbed my eyes and said, "I just moved in," as if he had accused me of something.

The landlord said, "Maybe I should run upstairs and get you some."

I saw that he was ready to go to the door. "I don't want to put you to any trouble," I said.

With each second of him standing there hovering over me, I was feeling stickier and stickier.

The landlord said, "Well, how else are you going to clean this up?"

I hadn't considered it. I stared up at the bare bulb until I saw spots of light when I blinked.

"Go on," I said. "I guess I do need something," I said. **Q**

Top Dollar

Only the moonlight is Miami. Other than for the moonlight, this place could be anyplace—you know, the captain's chairs, the faded blue back wall hung with fishnets, the plastic lobsters on the fishnets, plus the plastic crabs. We are eating crab, some sort of giant crab I am supposed to like. "Enjoy your crab," the waiter says.

So I am supposed to eat crab, enjoying, and also to talk. We, my husband and I, are the ones who are supposed to talk. All the old man can do is wheeze. His wheeze is as pervasive as the Miami moonlight. Everywhere, moonlight wheezes. Everywhere, Miami wheezes. I suspect the crab.

Crab is what the old man says he wants before he wheezes his last. Crab is on his wish list. "Crab," he wheezes, so we are here eating crab in this place famous for crab, all of us, me, the old man, and my husband, who is the son of the old man, all three of us are eating the special *specialité,* God knows how many bucks' worth of crab; not that money matters at a time like this, not when the old man looks wasted by moonlight, not when the old man wanes.

I myself do not want to eat crab. I myself do not even like crab. I am here because my husband has asked me to be here. "Talk," my husband whispers while the old man wheezes. My husband says, "You can talk."

So here I am, eating crab and talking to the old man, which old man I have seen less of in my entire life than he has days left to live on this earth, if you believe the doctors who let him out to eat crab by moonlight with my husband, his son, who pays for it all and does not talk.

I talk about baseball, about Joe DiMaggio and Roy Campanella, and was it not too bad about Roy, and about how it must be hard for any of them to live that life when you know you have only so many years in you, and how some of them, those players, try to keep it going by playing all taped up, and it is me going on like this, this female me is talking like this, while my husband, the son with the season tickets he always told the old man to come up to New York and someday use someday, that husband and son sits silent.

I hear myself running out of baseball.

I hear the old man running out of wheeze. It is as if I can hear the old man's heart, which has grown too big and loose and sloppy, this heart that does not do enough of what a heart should do, that is not pumping enough, so that the old man's lungs are not pumping enough, so that these lungs are filling with fluid, so that the old man is always short of breath, like someone swimming who is not good at swimming, which is how the doctors described it to my husband, the son, and to me, when the doctors said that this old man's death will, in effect, be death by drowning. Drowning in moonlight, I am thinking, while I am talking baseball, while I am saying, "Who is that guy?"

"You know," I say to my husband, the son. "Who is that utility guy who plays all the time, head to toe almost, all taped up, so that people say you cannot tell whether it is the man playing baseball or only the tape?"

I see the old man's old black eyes fixed on the face of his son, as he tilts his old man's chin at an inquiring tilt, as if to say that he cares about what my husband, his son, has to say about utility players in tape.

The old man is wheezing worse than ever, but what I hear is how hard the old man is trying. I see the old man trying to have us not see that he has hardly eaten any of his crab, trying with both his elbows propped up on the table, his elbows on the table a way of merely being polite, of hiding how he does not eat his crab, and also because the propping of his elbows is what keeps him from falling. I see the old man trying not to die on us, not here, not now. I see the old man trying to last until dinner is over and he can go back to bed and die his death. I see the old man also until then, for now, as long as he has to, trying to hear what my husband, his son, will say, what name this son will name.

My husband, the son, says a name, some name, maybe the right name, maybe the wrong name, who knows? and then all that we, the old man and me, hear from my husband, his son, is the sound of his fish fork, pick, pick, pulling crabmeat out of the hard pink shell of a crab.

I blame moonlight. I think it must be the moonlight that makes me want to say what I want to say, that makes me wild to speak.

I talk about crab. I say that you cannot be too careful with crab, how I heard that a lot of restaurants are serving their customers dead, drowned crab. I say that drowned crab has to be dangerous.

"A crab is an aquatic animal," my husband, the son, says. He says that an aquatic animal such as a crab cannot drown.

I say there was this stuff on the water. I say that the stuff on the water was laid down like moonlight on water, and that it kept the oxygen out of the water, and without oxygen, the crabs, in effect, drowned. I say that I have heard that some restaurants are serving dead, drowned crab, and at top dollar.

My husband, the son, puts the crab leg back on his plate. "Why did you have to go ahead and say that?" he says. "Tell me why did you have to say that?"

It is the old man who speaks. Through the wheeze, I hear the old man tell his son, my husband, to eat. The old man says that the crab is fine, and the old man says this "fine" as if he still has the strength in him to bring his son a fine meal of crab. The old man says that where we are is a fine place and that the meal is a fine meal, and that it is not every day that we are all together in Miami in the moonlight, and that the where we are and the way we are together is fine. Then the old man says for me to talk. "Talk," the old man says. He orders talk. "Talk about us being here," he says. "Make it Miami." **Q**

The Violent Society

It was at the Noctambule before it reopened under its new, current management. Every Wednesday night, they dimmed the lights at 1 A.M. and brought out Fanny Jackson, the fat black striptease artist.

I stress that she was an artist.

I looked across the room, the way you do when you know what's coming, to see who else was in the know.

There was nothing sexy about Miss Fanny. There wasn't supposed to be. It was humiliation. She undressed to the beat, but quickly, to get that part over with. Meanwhile, the over-the-hill crowd danced next to the disconnected jukebox. The waiter flexed his arms and crossed them.

Miss Fanny had a gift, plucking the one curiosity seeker out of his chair and stripping him naked, slowly and with malice. That night it was a girl; better still.

"Hey!" the girl bleated, but her idiot boyfriend just smiled, like at a magic show.

The helpless girl was alone under the spots.

"Like my big black tits, honey?" Miss Fanny husked into the mike, low-voiced.

The crowd applauded, encouraging the girl. She smiled and nodded yes, she did like them.

"Then let's see yours!"

First the top. Then the rest. The girl was shivering under the spot, hands covering her pubic hair. The crowd had formed a buffer between the stage and her seated, uncertain, unsmiling boyfriend.

Thrilled, I bit deeply into my knuckle.

"No! No!" the girl screamed when Miss Fanny produced the dildo.

"Calm yourself, honey," Miss Fanny purred, and we laughed. Oh sure.

"You can't have *this*!" Miss Fanny exploded, laughing and rubbing the foot-long dong between her tits.

"Ah! Oh! Honey!" she exclaimed. "Look."

She bent at the knees and parted her massive thighs.

"Show us yours," Miss Fanny encouraged, saintly smiling. "Come on, don't be shy."

The girl backed away, toward the edge of the stage.

"Watch your step, honey," Miss Fanny warned.

As the girl looked over her shoulder, Miss Fanny took a quick step forward and pushed. The girl fell into a sea of helpful arms. And applause.

"Get the bird," I heard a voice.

They brought out a yellow-throated bird, as big as one of Miss Fanny's hands. The crowd hushed.

She slit the bird from beak to bowel, pulled out its stomach, and threw it at the first wave of well-wishers. They dove under the upheld bird and let the blood fall on their cheeks.

I hadn't known birds could hold so much.

I went into business with my brother. He was a lot older than me and, according to my parents, a bad influence. I never understood that either. Like polluted water?

My first night of apprenticeship, I was hidden in a hotel closet with my eye up against the keyhole. I could smell the bed from there, and I could see half the room.

My brother brought in this sixty-year-old lady. Later, he swore she wasn't that old, but I can assure you she was.

She laughed a lot, because of what my brother said and how he said it. He was at the same time gallant and coarse, but had a kind of self-mocking swagger, as if the whole act were a wink. It wasn't Johnny, but she was laughing. I didn't know how she could fall for him.

I could see his hairy asshole so clearly, I started pulling at my underwear.

"Sex me," she whined, "oh, sex me," and then she breathed out like a goat—"Eeeh—eeeh—eeeh."

"Not so fast," Johnny moaned, "you're making me come." And she believed him. I swear.

His pants were crumpled around his ankles. I knew what his underwear looked like, so I wasn't surprised he wasn't wearing any. I took some notes.

Johnny and the lady both had on their platform shoes. That's another thing—he wore them for real, and he thought they were still cool. Maybe when you do time, you lose track of fashions.

Since Johnny was raking in a lot of money, he didn't make me pay rent. We shared a big room in a Jackson Heights flophouse.

When things weren't so good, we stole olives and peanut butter from the A&P across Northern Boulevard.

One other thing, not that I think it means anything. When he didn't have a girl over, we shared the bed. Otherwise, I slept on a blanket in a corner.

"Ernest?" he mumbled. "Where the fuck did we end up last night?"

"Here," I said, turning over on my back.

"Didn't we get any girls?"

"Yeah. We fucked them in the redhead's car."

"I thought so. How you feel?"

"Okay."

"I think I got it again."

"Shit."

"Fuck."

"Shit."

When Johnny got the syph, we didn't have a lot of money.

Johnny copped a medical discharge from the U.S. Navy. It went like this:

NAVY SHRINK: You admit knowing what you did is wrong?
JOHNNY: I do.

My mother sent me a note warning me about Johnny. She sent it to our room, and she still figured he wouldn't read it.

The evil guy was slender and cultivated, and he wore a dandy diamond in a gaudy gold setting. I stared at the fork on the table and thought about sinking it in the soft spot between his eyes.

But Johnny said, You can count on me, and I didn't want to let him down. I had a highly developed sense of responsibility. At least on a par with my flight instinct.

I didn't have to do anything I didn't feel comfortable doing. That was the deal. Of course, I couldn't lose the mark. So I had to do certain things, perhaps. Simple things, like be a wallflower, listen to hear if a certain combination of words were spoken, not even listen, just hear, just be a human tuning fork. I was told what the words were. I had to hear them.

Then there was the letter; it went like this:

DEAR MR. JABLONSKI,
As you know, we have been compiling the *Compleate* JABLONSKY *Family Encyclopedia* for several years. It includes the different branches of the JABLONSKI clan, the several waves of JABLONSKI American Emigration, the various noble titles held by the JABLONSKI name (and includes those that still do bear the JABLONSKY emblem!).

We've asked our printer to reserve 500 copies for libraries and specialized bookstores across the country. To order your own copies at reduced prices, to ensure that you have the *Compleate* JABLONSKI *Family Encyclopaedia* in your home, fill out the coupon below.

With me working now, and with Johnny's letter, we were raking in the money. But we kept the room, anyway. I don't think either one of us got a special thrill out of it. It was more likely a precaution against bad times. We both faced toward the middle of the bed.

I told Johnny I didn't think I could handle all of the details of the job.

"Ernest, you got to trust me," he said.

Johnny had been through a lot. The sixties. Platform shoes. He must know, I thought.

The cultivated man and Johnny and I were walking east, in full public view, in Greenwich Village. But a lot can happen, even in public, east. Which is what happened. Mr. Cultivated spins around and hits me with the back side of his hand, precisely with that V-shaped, sharpened-for-just-this-purpose diamond. A cut opens up that wouldn't close. I began to bleed what they call profusely.

"Lay off my brother," Johnny said. "Please."

Cultivated said, "You want to take it for him, Johnny?"

"Okay," Johnny said.

I leaned against a car, pressing my sleeve against the cut. I didn't know that when they rub sugar in your cut, it doesn't heal so fast.

Johnny was ripped like a red pinstripe shirt. His earring was pulled out of his ear.

Meat, meat, meat.

I watched like it was funny. When Cultivated was gone, Johnny said, "Better me than you, right?"

Later that week, Johnny was booked for mail fraud.

I was sitting in the Noctambule one afternoon, and the new owners were busy tossing new chairs and tables around like politicians making promises. I'd heard they'd been looking to get a good deal on the place—nobody wanted to see that kind of garbage anymore.

Beats me.

I would pay two-fifty for a beer any night Fanny Jackson is up.

Johnny got ten-to-twenty in the violent society. **Q**

May

After I got back (gone six days), slept late. Could tell sky was blue outside (May, flowers, birds building what birds build), but I was tired and so I kept going back to sleep. So slept until ten-thirty. She had picked me up at the airport in Spokane, and we didn't get back until around three in the morning, and then we had not gotten off to sleep until around daylight. She had to be at the school to teach by eight—she set the alarm for seven—but it turned out they had called off school today because no one showed up. There are only seven children in the school, and on a day in May like this, they often cut out and go off down the Yaak River, strung out all up and down the river as if seining—the smallest ones catching tad-poles by scooping them up with coffee cups, and the oldest, the boys using cane poles for trout. There are big trout in the Yaak, wild lilies growing yellow all along either shore. You can see that on a hot day there's no other choice.

She brought my breakfast upstairs—grits, eggs, bacon, hash browns, toast with huckleberry jelly, and coffee. She sat behind me on the big bed and touched my back as I ate.

It's woods and wilderness all around us, all the way up into Canada, and beyond. There's going to be a ban on logging in these woods this summer. The whole valley will be silent.

Early in the afternoon, she went up the road to play pi-nochle with her pals. I came out into the yard and lay down on a blanket in the tall blowing wind-flattened grass, with the sun hot on me, and me wearing sunglasses I'd fashioned for myself out of a coat hanger and some shady green plastic.

I balanced the checkbook—did feats of magic with it, play-ing with such small numbers. **Q**

See the Dog

I think the kindest part of the story is that I did not remember them waking me up in the middle of the night.

O, Buddha! Oh, for the man who stands on the hillside perched on one leg. Oh, for the wine and the life of abstention.

The man on one leg looks out over the landscape. What is there to see that would match the attention of living on one leg?

Heaven, cries the Buddha. Just look, there is everything. You've heard it all before—the blade of grass, its complex strategy of taking in water, its greening.

I rise from the subway into April's crazy bloom. Here is the dangle of wisteria; here the yellow kerchief flowering on a woman's head. Here, in a satin baseball jacket, her son's arms are like waxy stems. Here are the carefully potted tulips; here, tight pink jeans cover a teenager's petal thighs. Here the pudgy grapes, the grocer's bouquet of radishes.

My sweetest love, this is my confession—today I love all the junk of the world and somehow love it all equally; resisting nothing, I love neon, synthetics, polyester, magenta rhinestones.

Now the orange letters above the dry cleaner's seem rare as a florist's exotica.

He wobbles a little, you would, too.

He does not think every blade of grass or every curve of hillside is a gorgeous event.

I whistle and I get in trouble with the ladies. Of course, I was whistling at them.

. . .

I am trying to concentrate on calamity. I am trying to call back everything I know about the scourge that is history, but I am distracted by the sparrows clamoring and the alert faces of men betting three-card monte.

I will tell you the sorrow of the happy man. It is that I cannot resist wanting to know who is happier, the little piggy that went to market or the one that stayed home.

Look, I don't have to be Buddha to know that you breathe in and breathe out in either event.

I put my brush to the paper and begin. With the curved line I paint the mountain range; a swift stroke and the waterfall starts down; at the bottom, a wind rises from the green forest and the foaming water rushes in a stream.

See the man, the blunt stroke of his body; he does not wobble in the painting.

Love, pity the happy man—the mountain range is large and the pupil of the eye small. I want to hold it close, within an inch of my eye, but then I do not see its form.

Ah, there. At a distance, a distance of, say, seven miles, I enclose the mountain within the square inch of my pupil.

Now I drain the wine cup, play the lute, lay down the picture of scenery, face it with silence, tracking the four borders to wilderness. Here are the cliffs and the peaks; here the grove; here, stretching out of the mist, is the walkway with its split-rail fence.

Split-rail fence!—someone has been here before me.

How does the happy man pray? He prays like all other men, with the board of directors compiling an agenda in his heart.

It begins to drizzle, drops connecting on the sidewalk.

I am worried for him, stuck out in the rain, on one determined but unsteady leg. I want to bring him for this part, towel him dry, promise him that tomorrow will arrive and with it a good, sunny day for perching. How can he not be tempted; the one leg aches and the other is bored and yearns to be set down.

That is the amazement, that the raised leg is not content to give up its burden and go along on a free ride.

The rain keeps coming, drops falling in their angled plunge. Umbrellas open; water collects in the cup of the tulip; ladies gather under awnings, waiting like girls at a firemen's ball.

Oh, girls, what could be happier than the happy man in an April shower?

See the dog out in the rain. See the dog sniff and wag its dog tail. See the dog absorbed in the precise situation of its present life.

The sparrows move in a single great flush. One tree to the next. They settle on a branch as if they might stick around for a while, and then they're off. In the center of the sparrows, a tropical shock of green. I look up. Where is the woman leaning halfway out her window calling for her pet parakeet to come home? Where is the hand waving a branch of fresh millet?

O God-of-Happily-Ever-After, hear me out. I am like any other man in this unwieldy garden. Mine is happiness, his is shame.

Abundance, abundance, abundance.

Still, I am dying. **Q**

Sonority

You never see Ann really let herself dance; in lieu of it, she gives little imitations. These last a couple of seconds at a time. She rattles her head like pills to the power chords, agreeing with nothing. Choking on volts. But she comes out of it each time sighing, a pleased smile under her long, clever nose. "That kind of dance," she says. "That pantomime, locking out time. That's what you do." *Me?* I pretend to search myself. I don't want to know "what you do." I want Ann just to do it. Instead, she has another two-second attack. She holds an imaginary mike to the chins of some bewildered, thrashing kids and pulls away laughing. Then she runs across the dance floor to me, her dark bangs flying, and steals the notepad from my coat. *Fighting the music,* she writes, *because you don't want it to end*—flashes it once in my face like a credential; I'm still seeing the words after the pad is tucked away. *Fighting the music.* I touch Ann's hair, savoring the nice description.

Apparently Ann likes the line too, because twenty minutes later I overhear her using it on Chuck. (Chuck is this band manager Ann wants to impress; he recently hired her to design some album covers.) Not that I have to eavesdrop. Ann doesn't mind if I know everything about her, all her plans and designs. Or she tells herself that in some sense I already do, a concept she considers a relief. Letting one friend in on her sins is Ann's compromise with guilt. The thought of one person "understanding." I fell into the role by what seems like a ludicrous coincidence. Someone had given me a religious pamphlet called *Understanding,* and I was trying it out. That isn't the gist of a story—it is the whole story. I remember the pamphlet almost photographically. "Understanding Evil," "Understanding Famine," "Understanding Perplexity," and what seemed to be a high number of cartoon illustrations, leaping with question marks: Understanding was the answer to it all. This was last fall, in Los Angeles—"The autumn of your Christ-like stare," my brother calls it. I would read my pamphlet and my newspaper over hot-and-sour soup at Chao Praya, world events rolling off my shoulders. One day, Ann walked in irritably and asked if I thought I could share. I offered her the View section and she said, *The table.*

People are always surprised to find out I'm younger than Ann—by three months, but younger just the same—because I act so comparatively reserved. I'm not sure what to make of that analysis; I used to strike people as "defeated," so possibly it is a move up. It seems to me that from the start Ann and I were equally tired, but of different things. She was tired of defending herself, and I was tired of my expectations. I was tired of voting even, if that relates, it was the first year I didn't register, although I made the mistake of keeping a tally, and all my causes and candidates lost, except for one initiative, which according to an exit poll a majority of voters misunderstood on account of a double negative. There is a point where hopelessness and strength look like the same thing to me. Four, five days into our Chao Praya phase, Ann was working herself up, reading me her stone-faced riot act, warning me she was a disaster, and sad, and a cheat, and no friend of mine, and on about some vitamins she'd been stealing from her roommate just to see if he'd forgive her; she had eaten three multi-tabs already today.

What I did was throw my wallet on the table. My wallet and then my car keys, and the pamphlet, too. I just pushed it all across the table and touched Ann's hair (our first time). I kept hearing the voice of a television car salesman: I will eat my tie, I will stand on my head and stack dimes at the corner of Sunset and Vine. It was supposed to be a powerful stunt, my renunciation of things material. I wanted to say, "It's all right." But then the words seemed overly literal, and I was stuck there with my hand through the leaves of a centerpiece, smoothing Ann's bangs and wondering all at once how it was, how it actually was that people talked to each other. It's hard to describe the gravity of what I was feeling—that sense of injustice all tied up with love. It was less a matter of loving Ann than an almost anonymous love wish for her, wanting Ann to feel loved without me in the way. And all the trite futility of that.

Which at any rate has made us a kind of tragic marvel in the eyes of our friends, a modern Jake and Brett. For the record, I don't like being told that what I've been doing all these months with Ann is protecting myself, that when I say I don't want to demand things of Ann, I supposedly mean I don't want to care. Generally the unspoken topic here is sex. At about three months, I think it was, sex became an option for us. Just an option, and then it seemed to stop. What had made it possible in the first place was the innocence: Ann was crying about something that frightened her, a medical scare one of her sisters had had—Ann didn't even know how scared she'd been until it turned out to be a false alarm—and I was holding her, by her kitchen sink, feeling so young and ordinary and loyal; it was a hot day and Ann's cheek was tear-streaked, her face broken out, and just for a moment it seemed (paradoxically) erotic to think that there was nothing separating us, that nothing held a sexual charge.

Then the phone rang in the hall and it was Ann's friend Helen, this publicist who throws terrible theme parties. Helen is the biggest matchmaker of the bunch. ("Is that who I think it is, coughing in the background?") I guess the popular demand finally killed it for us. Ann made a joke, about how she could do absolutely anything she put her mind to, until she thought it was required of her.

Back then, Ann couldn't bring herself to show this guy Chuck her artwork. She was reluctant even to approach him in Helen's back yard and hand him a business card (on Pearl Harbor day—a Luau). The alibi was always college: Ann felt she had been cheated of something essential, some notion of a training ground for adulthood, because after both her older sisters went through Berkeley, the money ran out; her father got sick. Ann was only eight and got her image of higher education from the pictures in her sisters' yearbooks: For years she thought you had to wear the mortarboards to class. My question was, What *wasn't* a training ground, when you thought about it? I confronted Ann, there in the moonlight, at Helen's. What made her think life was anything but? "It's all Berkeley," I said. "Think of it as Berkeley." I can get a little electrified sometimes—a transformation that makes Ann practically applaud, bouncing on a sofa and disregarding on the spot the substance of whatever it is I'm talking about. When Chuck finally appeared, all the tension had gone. Ann glided over to him in her grass skirt and presented her card, as kindly and effortlessly as if it were a scrap he had dropped and she was returning. I watched from across the lawn, feeling a certain pulse of empathy, trying to decide if she was using the Berkeley trick. Wondering if that was what leveled her out. And later she told me yeah, she guessed so, although just our dialogue had helped, too: the ritual of speech, some constancy in the night. It sort of grounded her. Did I know what she meant?

The plan now is to leave the club and head over to the West Hollywood motel where Chuck and the band, called The Hellionz, are staying. There, they intend to discuss Ann's idea for their album cover. I've just received this news from the drummer, Evan, who has the assignment of giving me a ride, since Ann has already met up with the others backstage. Evan and I are the only two left in the club. Nevertheless, it has taken him three approaches on foot to convince himself I'm his man. I'm leaning back against the bar, wearing a blue blazer I bought specifically for a *Sports Illustrated* party earlier today, which makes me look as if I am in the Secret Service. Evan is wearing a black undershirt and has his hair tied so that it points straight up, in a single frond. For the past few minutes I've been adjusting my cuffs, studying my grip on a soda glass, and Evan has been passing back and forth in front of me, like something in a shooting gallery.

Evan starts the engine in the rented four-door Chevette and then clicks it off again. "Look," he says uncomfortably. "Do you mind if I smoke?"

He means a Marlboro. He smokes one all the way down, flicking the ashes out the window into the alleyway. It's a warm night, no snap in the air at all. One last deep drag and we're on our way. "The others won't let me smoke in the motel room," Evan says. "And Chuck tells me that if you get in an accident in California and the police find out you were smoking, your insurance won't cover you. It's insane. I smoke cigarettes; you'd think I was some kind of *fiend.*" We ride over a bump and the top of his frond smashes up against the ceiling.

"He's pulling your leg," I say.

"Who?"

"Chuck. About the insurance laws."

Evan looks at me, and then he says, "Rock and roll isn't like it was. Nowadays it's people like Chuck. Nobody is straight with anybody else." He adjusts the rearview. "You used to know who you could trust by their music."

"I really don't know what the spirit of the joke was," I say.

Evan shrugs. "I take everything too seriously," he says.

In the motel room, The Hellionz all frown over their drinks, lukewarm vodka and grapefruit juice in plastic bathroom cups. I volunteer to get some ice down the hall, but Evan calls after me when I reach the machine, which I discover is padlocked. "You need—it's complicated." He isn't kidding. Beside the lock is a typed 5×7 index card headed, SUBJECT: ICE PRIVILEGES. "They make you borrow a key," Evan explains, steering me down a covered walkway to the front office. It's a 1960s-style motel, stairwell railings painted the colors of tropical fruit, and clean, but the windows are barred and there are hints of a new, bureaucratic embattlement; management cannot seem to invent house rules fast enough. At poolside, ten rules came with the preprinted sign, and two more have been added with a felt marker: *Number 11, Deposit Room Key to Use Pool Light,* and *Number 12, No Marco Polo.*

"I wonder if Marco Polo ever played Marco Polo," Chuck is joking, later. One eyebrow dances around. The "business session" has lasted ten minutes at most; Evan and I barely had time to pack the bathroom sink with ice. Now everyone has retired to the pool area.

Chuck is drunk. He lies on his back on a patch of lawn, calling out the names of constellations, a cup of vodka balanced on his solar plexus. When I walk by, he says hello without breaking his rhythm. "Pegasus, Capricorn, Ann's friend," he says. It's easy to see how Chuck's personality could get irritating, at least to Evan; but he has his charming side, too, if you're not relying on him to take anything seriously (and I'm not). By instinct he's a lovable drunk. If he says something sarcastic, he follows it by crossing his eyes at his drink, so that the joke is on him, too. Plus a repertoire of faces. The best is the one he wears to say he simply loves something; he shuts his eyes and smiles in a way that looks as if everybody is pouring champagne over his head. He loved Ann's cover concept that much, or he claimed to, which is how the meeting ended almost as soon as it began. One second Chuck's face was blank, looking at Ann's rough sketch (a visual pun, The Hellionz were tied together in a green bunch, like scallions); the next, it's raining champagne. I LOVE IT, Chuck roared, crouching in the middle of the room, eyes shut tight. Ann just looked over at me, dumbfounded, mouthed a question: "What are we going to do now?"

What we are going to do now, in response to the fact that nobody has brought a bathing suit, is something that strikes Chuck as a priceless inspiration. We are going to play Marco Polo without the pool. Close your eyes, crawl on elbows, lunge at each other's whispers in the grass. What do we all think? Chuck scans the faces, beaming. That about does it for Evan; he gathers up his cigarettes and heads inside to write some postcards home. He asks how we all stand the level of intellect.

I don't know: personally I'm feeling relieved at Chuck's idea. I was worried that everyone was going to want to go skinny-dipping. I thought I was going to have to watch Ann stand there by the Coke machine and weigh the proposition, what it would mean if you were the only female and everyone was drunk and now you were taking off your clothes with The Hellionz. Thoughts like that. Not that Ann's behavior is any of my business. Weird that I should have to coach myself to remember something so fundamental. Things feel almost too alive tonight, neuralgic; the blades of grass superstitious and bare. I look at Ann, see a certain glow about her, and suddenly I could practically hate her for liking it as she might, the approval of these guys. Uncaring guys, fair-weather guys, guys she cannot possibly disappoint. I say this even though I've been like them before. Certainly I've been Chuck. I wonder what I resent.

And the resentment is so childish, I can only forgive myself for it, and the rest of them, too. I'm patting the grass with my palm now, just to feel it spring back; just to do something with my mood. Ann, meanwhile, has declared herself "it." She hurls herself to the middle of the lawn, covers her eyes with her arm, begins counting backward from twenty, out loud, uncovers one eye. Even in that role, she's no child, exactly; she's a thirty-year-old woman playing a game—she shoots a reproving eye at all of us, as if to remind us of the fact. But there is an innocence to her just the same. An expression I've seen before. I'm looking up at the stars, remembering a time. We were at a concert and the lights had gone down and Ann went into a truly giddy act, started pretending the rush of camera fire in the arena was all for her. She was whipping her ponytail in it, skipping up the stairs in the colonnade. Lights popping all around her, a kind of lovesick sky.

She looks the same way now. Unfortunately, none of us has turned out to be terribly clear on how Marco Polo is played, with or without the pool. The result is that Ann is calling out "Marco," perched like a mantis, and the rest of us are shrugging uselessly at each other from opposite corners of the lawn. A long, awkward silence, and then, just as awkwardly, Chuck and I rush to fill it, chirping out *Po-lo* at exactly the same time, and with our voices in something too close to harmony. This paralyzes Ann. She tilts her head one way and the other, toward Chuck and toward me; then she just cracks up, flops on her side. End of game. Chuck yells foul, throws his plastic cup overhead; Ann wipes her eyes, basking in the lame coincidence. "That didn't count!" She laughs.

I go to bed still thinking about Ann's voice, which I've decided is extraordinary—the kind of voice I'd entertain myself with if it were mine; lie in the dark and test it, marvel at its honest weight in the room. Ann must know. She doesn't even mind hearing herself on tape, and a couple of times I've seen her play back my answering machine, intrigued. I can tell by watching her that she hears the same things I do, the layers. The young, scholastic quality, first off; the kid genius. Which must have been a curse to her at one point or another, the kind of thing grownups make a fuss over. Perhaps in response she has this other, worldlier tone, its own commentary, a voice that's a little tired of itself and yet more tired of trying to be anything different. It's the sober, lovely voice of a woman at the end of a day.

The month Ann left Seattle, I was asking Charla for a divorce. I drank a pint of Scotch to work up to the ceremony, sitting hunch-shouldered on a nicked piano bench. "I'm going to miss nights like this," I said. "You're wondering what I mean." The anesthetic had settled in and I was grinning and the scene deteriorated. Across the room, I watched my wife moving her lips. Gesticulating—like something under a glass. Which I suppose was the effect I was after, though it horrifies me to look back.

Ann was working paste-up in the ad department of a Seattle indie record company, trusting her luck for the first time since her father died. She couldn't even name what had changed for her; she kept looking for something to thank. She strung a Casper kite overhead and named it McGhost. She was the first one at work every day. She liked everything about the job: the neatness of the work; the deft, styptic action of her wrists with an X-acto; the long hours on her feet (a good way around her big creative fear, which was Sitting Down to Work). Management gathered in doorways to watch her. The president gave her an office key.

Within a month the ax fell. Ann started using the key to steal typesetting supplies. This was fairly common in her field, but Ann didn't even try to cover it. When the boss caught on, she shrugged. She reminded him he was the founder of an "alternative label." He said she was fired, and absolutely without disrespect, Ann responded, No, you can't. Each thought the other was joking. By the time the whole thing ended, she'd made a scene. She tore down the kite and ran with it, she told me, a battered flight through the Seattle office, howling No.

For me that image holds a certain echo, a false déjà vu—as though I ought to be able to recall myself being there, playing some obvious role in Ann's life. Like memory, but with the carefully spooked air of a doctored photo. I'll see myself at the company picnics, or napping in a chair by her drawing board. I don't see myself at all when she's having her disaster at the record company, but I seem to see my absence; in fact, I'd swear by the look on her face that Ann is wondering where on earth I could be.

It's a short leap from all of this to My Theory—that Ann had been sending me extrasensory smoke signals across time—and around sundown I decide to get out of the apartment and go tell her about it. I expect she's in her studio with the stereo on, doing The Hellionz design. But she doesn't come to the door when I arrive, and I don't hear music inside.

There's that deadpan moment after an unanswered doorbell, the solid recognition of an obstacle. *Our souls are one, but I missed you at home.* I hear the dueling low dispute of a leaf blower far off with the whoosh of a car going by. It's a good sunset: Ann could be at the beach. I take a step back toward my car, and stop, because behind me Ann has opened the front door.

She wears stiff Levi's with a white T-shirt that shrunk too much in the shoulders and tugs at her bra; her hair is clipped back except for the bangs. She is all face, with brown bangs, looking at me as if a marginal joke has been told and she'll agree to laugh if I will. "Well?" she says. A broad smile going now. She means last night. I'm her reality check: she wants to know what I thought of it all. I'm following her upstairs, tossing her ponytail in my hand, and when I've taken too long to reply, she changes the question. What did I think of Chuck? This time I interrupt her and surprise myself. I kiss her square on the mouth.

And no sooner do I pull away than the separation feels unjust. Something stirs in me, solemn and fundamental. How long have I wanted Ann?

It's like this: When Ann tells me she slept with Chuck last night, I can't help it; I look away and jut my lip. This makes her ask what's wrong and I can't even tell her. I pretend there's a principle involved. I tell her Chuck is a creep; I tell her my opinion of her is damaged. Every name I think of to call Ann gives the thing more power instead of less, and when she tries to soothe me, it's worse. It was the mood, it was an impulse, it was "Berkeley," she says in the goddamn Ann voice and I run to the car, all her smart-neurotic protests following me downstairs.

So give me one night to get myself together. It's not as if we can't still be friends.

What's funny is the sounds you hear when you just stop thinking for a while. The Hellionz are on the turntable with the volume off, a flat midget screech living in the vinyl. Outside, I've got crickets, millions maybe—the back yard throbs—crouching beside their own dry ritual noise.

Ann says this all night to my phone machine: "Come on. Are you there?" Some static. "Oh, man—I know someone's there." Q

Lady

She said *please.* Her face looked something more than bitter, with hair which it turned out was a hat, which came down over her ears, which was made of fake fur, which she never removed from her head. She had glasses on. Everything she wore helped me decide to let her in.

She wore flat black patent-leather shoes with pointed toes, with black stockings, wrinkled at the ankles, with silver triangles set in on top of the toes of the shoes, and she had on a long black coat, and she was shorter than I am.

Her skin was a bleak sort of skin, and there was no beauty left in her—maybe in her whole body.

I felt that this lady was fast, because she was at the place where I keep my red rotary-dial phone before I was, after I said, "The phone is in here."

She said, "I know the number."

Sitting on the arm of my sofa, she dialed while her knees were knocking into and tipping back onto two legs my too small table, which my phone sits on; and my oversized brass lamp, which sits on the table, too, with the huge shade, might have crashed. The lamp was clanging, ready to go. She got it back.

She said, "MERLA!" into the phone receiver.

I knew it—she must have known it—Merla knew it, too, that Merla was only a matter of one hundred to two hundred yards from my house, because this woman I had let in, she had told me right off the house number she was looking for. She was telling Merla that it was *impossible* to get to her, that there was no way on earth, that she had kept on running into this east-west street.

"A nice picture," she said to me. She had gotten herself up. She was looking at all those men dressed for one of the dark-age centuries, marching through foliage, trekking around a hunched-up woman at a well, with their weird insignias on their chests that nobody I know can figure out, with their faces—version after version of the same face.

She said, "I have a (something something) reproduction—" I cannot remember the dates or the royal reign to which she referred, when she was toying with this miniature chair that I have, grabbing it by its arm and swiveling it on the clubbed foot of one leg, as she was leaving, after everything had been agreed upon with Merla. She would not be getting out of her car for Merla. Merla would meet her at the corner, Merla would.

She, the lady, must have been curious or put off by the jumble of dirty things at my front door that I suppose she first noticed when she was leaving, or by the splendor of my living room just off from the jumble. She missed going inside of it to see what was going on in each of the pictures in there.

What this woman had done to me was incalculable, and she had done it all in a period of time which had lasted no more, I am sure, than five minutes, which so many others have done, coming in here only for the telephone, because I had waved at her while she was shouting at Merla; I had said, "Would it help you to know the number of *this* house?"

Then I had told this little person my wrong address, but not because I wanted to, or because of any need on my part to make up a lie.

I said 270, which is way off the track, except for two digits, but I had rearranged them, the 7 and the 0, but I did not know I had done that. All that I knew was that I had done something unforgivably uncivil.

It was a lapse to reckon with. I took her into my arms, so that she could never leave me, and then jammed her up into the corner with the jumble by the front door and held her there, exhausting myself to keep her in there.

Violence is never the problem. Love at first sight is. **Q**

To Die

I undressed myself. I wanted sex—I wanted sex—I wanted sex—I wanted sex.

I climbed into my bed with my wife.

She wanted sex with me. She always wants sex with me.

When I discharged myself this time into her, I was feeling the banging of my organ up as high into her as I have ever gotten myself up into her.

I had just done the same with another woman who always wants sex with me, too.

There is another woman that I do the same with.

There is another woman.

There is another woman. There are five women who always want sex with me. They are always ready. It does not matter when or what or where, they are ready.

I have a great deal of money, which I have earned. I have physical beauty for a man. I have intelligence. I have work to do which I love to do, but women are what I prefer to anything: to lie down with them, the turning to touch the woman and knowing I will be received for sex as soon as I wish to be welcome.

I have been at it like this, this way for years. It does not matter when I die. I have had everything I ever wanted.

I should die now.

There should be a killing at my house.

There should be much, so much more for me, which I am not able to conceive of. **Q**

Egg

She had never allowed any egg of hers to get into such a condition, looking unlike itself and bulging, which was why the egg had all her attention from where it was in the depth of the sink, and from the depth of where it had been all dark yellow in the bowl, which had not been very far down inside the bowl, for there was no depth of anything inside the bowl, no particular depths of anything in either of her kitchen sinks either.

When she walked off from the sinks, thinking of the egg— "How unlike itself!"—she heard a yell, which was noise produced by standing water which was falling suddenly down deeply into the pipes below the sinks.

Variously, this yell was a choke to her, a slap, or the end of a life, so that she stopped when she heard the yell with her back to the sinks. She had the impression of a preamble.

This is the beginning of something.

She went and got another bad egg and gave it to the dog to eat out of the bowl, so that the bowl was scoured and banged about.

The dog, she thinks, gets everything, she was thinking later, walking the dog. He gets it, but pisses it and craps it away—daily—everything, and yet everyone shows the dog all their love.

Even she loves and she loves and she loves the dog.

The dog goes along down the street and the people say to her, "What a nice dog," and, "That's a nice-looking dog you've got there!" The dog takes her farther down the street than she intended to go, where then she is murdered.

The murderer loves and he loves the woman's dog for the rest of the dog's life. The dog loves the murderer in return. It is not a love that would stoop to being sexual. **Q**

Ultimate Object

She did not know there would be a cupboard full of vases, but she had had a hunch, as when her tongue on someone's skin could give her a hunch of what would happen. Let me repeat—a tongue on someone's skin.

She was with a friend with whom she could share her joy that there was a cupboardful. She said, "We're okay! They've got everything we could ask for!"

She was crouched, flat-footed, her body nearly into a ball, except for her neck and for her head not conforming, so that she could look into the cupboard to let all the joy which was packed inside the cupboard for her into her.

One plastic vase with a bulb shape, with a narrow tube protruding from the bulb upward, was light as a feather, and was as warm as plastic is.

One glass vase, the shape of a torso, was covered all over with rough-grained glass, when she took it out.

She did not let her friend take vases away when she held up vases to prove they were unsuitable because she pronounced it was so.

Each time she went down, to look in, the quality of the joy was as good, did as much for her—four times.

It was festivity.

And to her, it was festivity, the cooking or the heating, that the man who had nothing to do with either her or her friend was doing nearby at the stove.

His peaceable plan—to lift and to unfurl flat, round, yellow, black-speckled cakes—was the only other romantic transformation—not the product of imagination—going on in the place at the same time. And the man had no more right to be in this place—he was on the same shaky ground as she was, and as her friend was, by being there—which she saw him confirm with a smile she thought looked so easy for him to do.

It did not occur to her to get close to the man, to make an advance to taste, to do anything at all consequential vis-à-vis the man.

At the risk of startling readers, I will tell you that there was a dead body hidden not far from the man, which was the body of a woman the man had killed the day before, with a sharp-enough knife, then lying—the knife was—in a drawer above the cupboard of vases.

The woman's naked, somewhat hacked body, decapitated and frozen, was in the institutional-sized freezer adjacent to the stove. Out of her swollen face, her tongue protruded.

The wrong door, for all time, had been opened. **Q**

The Hounding

I had the Pontiac jacked up in the street in front of the house, changing out the front wheel-bearings, when I saw these two guys coming my way down the sidewalk. The one in front was carrying a big stick that looked to me like a piece of a tree limb with a knob on the end of it, whereas the other one had a brick.

Let me back up a minute and just say one thing. I love Krissy, but she says I think too much about the wrong things and not enough about what matters. I think Krissy is full of shit—I think she's the one with the problem. But there is no telling her that. Anyway, like I was about to say, something happened a couple of days ago that I can't stop thinking about. It's like trying to keep running from something that's chasing you in a dream.

Okay, it was late Sunday afternoon—right about the time when you get hit with that feeling of a weekend ending before it really got started, and another week about to start with the same motions to go through. I usually try to get busy doing something around the house when a feeling like this comes. Takes my mind off it. Like I said, I had the car jacked up and I was trying to get the inside bearing to slide all the way over the hub shaft. I had grease up to my elbows and I was about to take a hammer to it. But I told myself—calm down, take a deep breath, and just sit for a minute. It was cool out. The ground was cold where I was sitting, and yellow leaves from the hackberry tree kept drifting down and hiding my tools. And that's when I saw these two guys. They were Mexican boys, I think. They were walking about fifty feet apart. The one bringing up the rear—the one with the brick—I could see was skinny and had bad skin, and the one in front was shorter and stockier and walked with his head half-turned to the side so he could keep an eye on the guy behind him. They kept such an even pace they hardly seemed to move—it was more like the neighborhood was moving past them, half-disappearing, you might say.

Hey, all kinds of people come through here since there's so many rent properties all around—Krissy never lets me forget that it was my idea to get a real bargain on a house here. She says things like: "I might have known that you would carry me across the threshold of a house just emptied by white flight." You see how Krissy is always using her vocabulary on me? But what really caught my attention about these two boys was their expressions. They looked almost calm, but it was like a fierce kind of calm. It looked to me like the only thing they were seeing was each other. They didn't even look at me when they passed. And then, ever so slightly, something changed. It was a hesitation in the step of the boy in the back, and then suddenly he went into this kind of skip-run like an athlete setting up for a go at the high jump, while at the same time the stocky boy began to run—fast for his size—while the guy behind him, with all his strength, was throwing the brick at him. I held my breath. I could see the brick sail. But the timing of everything was such that the brick fell just about three feet short, bounced on the sidewalk almost up to the runner's heels, and then skittered off onto somebody's lawn. Whereupon the boy in front slowed down to a walk, and the boy in back went just fast enough to retrieve his brick and take up his position again. So far as I could hear, there was never a word said the whole time. I sat looking after them for a long time, and before they turned the corner, way down at the end of the street, I saw the kid in back get in three more tries with the brick. But the kid in front always saw it coming and always managed to be two, three steps ahead, so far as I could see.

Finally I looked up at Krissy—she was on the porch watering her leggy begonias—and I said, "Krissy, did you see that?" "See what?" she said. Krissy never looks up when she says that. So I asked her didn't she think it was time for her to go in and fry the potatoes. But she just gives me this look like she gets when she finds a big horn worm working over one of her tomato plants, so I knew I'd better just back off a little.

I got back to work, and after a while I get the brake drum back on, and the wheel, and I give it a few spins. I listen to the snick and glide of the bearings (I know I should have bought the kind that come in a box packed in grease), and every once in a while I look up and down the street. You see, I keep expecting to see these kids come around the block again. I couldn't figure what was so strange about what they were doing—I mean, after all, last week I saw a kid must've been about nine racing down the street pulling a little red wagon with a console TV on it. But there was something about this new thing that reminded me of something. I don't know what it reminded me of, but it seemed to be of a lot of things. I'm not making any sense, but you know what I mean. Anyway, it gets dark and I go in, but all evening long I keep thinking about what I'd seen. Lord knows, I couldn't explain it to Krissy. She was still mad at her mother, who'd called earlier and said I told you you couldn't grow dill in a hanging basket. Every time Krissy's mother calls I just say, "Hello, Mrs. Malroota, let me get Krissy for you." That woman has a real bulbous attitude.

I watched the news for a while. But it seemed crazier than ever—no sense to it, just lots of things being flashed on the screen. Well, so Krissy and I go to bed, and we hadn't been in there more than fifteen minutes or so when I hear something skitter outside. I jump up and look out through the blinds, but it must have just been a dry leaf scratching across the pavement. The moon was full and bright enough to make shadows, but there was nothing there that I could see. It gave me the shivers to think of those two boys out there walking around like two kids in an old black-and-white movie, chasing and running, chasing and running, like some machine. That's when Krissy all of a sudden says to me in the dark, "What the hell are you doing still up?" I didn't say anything. So after a minute she goes through this violent flop-turnover and clamps a pillow over her head.

I know if I'd said anything it would've been a fight.

I've learned.

I looked out again at all those shapes without color. The streets were empty. But I know the boys are still at it. I know there is no stopping them until something happens. **Q**

The Garden of the Emperor

He had come to the church garden with a camera, too restless to sit around the empty blue of the pool or to take a towel across the roadway to the beach to sit and watch the tankers plow the Gulf Stream to unknown destinations, passing and passing against the distant ratchet line of troubled blue, the same shape of ship passing by every time, moving without surprise, he thought, in the same far groove in the water.

It was a Sunday and the first fine day of sun for a week. The garden was open for visitors, and once he had eyed the cloistered courtyard and decided to save the film for something more than mullioned windows and climbing vines flowering purple and pink, what he saw through the stone archway leading into the garden was a long table set under an alcove, covered with a white tablecloth whose down-hung flaps were blowing in the breeze, and set with a large punch bowl filled with orange juice, the bulb of the clear ladle floating out in the middle of the orange lake like a small boat at anchor. At either side of the punch bowl were orange-colored paper cups, upside down in little towers. For the close shot, he focused on the little white folded-over card that said FOR OUR BRETHREN on it, and moving backward, what he was able to get into the frame was the potted palm in the corner, the arched wooden door behind the table with the iron-ring handle, and the wooden slats of the ceiling fan stuck up into a rafter like a huge thorn. He was tempted to move the tall wooden cross poled-up in the middle of the alcove facing the garden and put it somewhere in the composition, but he was afraid that someone might see him from the windows of the rector's office.

When the wind had settled, he shot the long view of what he thought looked like the Last Supper, set in the tropics, the towered cups waiting to be toppled by the thirsty Apostles, all the bad extras in this bad Hollywood film. Afterward, he walked circles around the cross, looking for the angle and the light, until it looked to him, through the lens, as if the tall wooden post with the beam spread out for arms was doing the moving, stalking the stalker, and stopping just when he stopped, like the killer always stops in old films when the person he is hunting down stops to look at his watch or to light a cigarette.

When he had dizzied himself restless looking for the shot that made sense, he ladled himself a paper cup of the orange juice, drank the juice in a gulp, and put the empty cup down onto the table, and headed for what he thought was the good light out there in the garden.

On the raised level a few cut-coral steps above the patio, he watched first one and then another of the little green lizards that darted in and out of the mint leaves flocked around the hedge bushes trimmed to cut the light into dark shadowed angles of the cross, bush after bush in a long row enfilading a matching set planted on the other side of the garden and looking to him like little raised graves. He kicked at the low border hedge and then listened for the rustle under the leaves. He ran his fingers over the flat top of one of the topiary bushes and then listened to the bristle sounds that the bush made. At the end of the row, he shot for perspective the dark cut green of the hedges that were crosses, rising out of the forest of lighter green like graves that had grown up out of the ground, pushed up from the bottom, he thought, by something underneath, or towering like green temples in an all-green world, kept to a trim by the small sharp teeth of the lizards.

To the sound of the organ echoing along the cloisters, he crept over the close-cut grass on the mound in front of the rector's office, dizzying the focus with every step to get closer to the little wooden house stilted up on a post, which looked to him to be a smaller version of the church, except for all the fancy gingerbread, all the carpenter's folly making it look like a Victorian pagoda for the birds, with its own devil dragon at the window. What he saw at the top of the little gingerbread steps, scaled down for something even smaller than a bird, he thought, with its feet clawed out on the little porch and on the wall of the house, and its chin resting on the sill of the cutout window, and its tail tapered out to the tip, was one of the dull green fat ones that he was thinking then might just be the true rulers out here in the all-green world outside the rector's window, just watching and waiting for their time to storm the temples of the world and live in the House of Man like wall-eyed emperors, making the windows their doors and the doors their windows.

While he was dizzying the focus, he saw the lizard poised at the sill slip quick as a shutter snap into the Chinese-devil house, the stiff gingerbread-carpentered dragons' tails trimming the gables, curling back upward upon themselves like ratcheted tongues of flame, and the long-necked shapes of dragons' heads propping up the corners of the eaves.

When he had it so that the light was coming into the little temple room in rayed rectangles and the focus was square to the edges, all that he could see of the lizard was the tail, coming out of the shadow of a corner like the wavy dagger of the assassin in some old black-and-white thriller, the little dragon god of the temple showing just the coattails of the master of the house, of these premises follied up for the birds. He pushed the shutter down and slipped out past the windows of the rector's office, through the stone arch trimmed to a point that he thought looked like a sharp-toothed bite out of this green hell or this green heaven, a man-sized gap carved out of the realm of this green emperor, pulsing in a corner.

In the cloister, he headed for the wooden rectangle of door at the end of the hallway that opened into the dark church. He headed for the sound of the organ, which he could hear droning through the leaded glass of the windows, dron-

ing out over the cut-coral stones of the courtyard, out over the
House of the Emperor, and out over the odd piece of carpenter's Gothic shoved back under the shade of the alcove, swept
clean to a splinter by every loose thief in the house, he
thought, by all those restless brother dragons of the cross. Q

New Baltimore Service Area

He pulled over because he was getting a little tired and he thought he might go to the bathroom, maybe get a candy bar and a Coke.

In the bathroom there was a guy, a janitor-type guy. The janitor guy was doing the sinks, one and then another—a little guy, maybe retarded. The janitor guy looked up from the sink he was doing and smiled: Hi.

He smiled back at the janitor guy: I appreciate what you're doing.

He went to a urinal, a medium one. There were the kiddie ones and then, I don't know, teenage ones, and grownup ones. He figured he was at a teenage one. It was nice to have different sizes. He looked down, the strong deodorizer, and little sneaker prints on the sides: a father holding his little son up to pee. A wonderful image filled with love.

The janitor guy had finished only one sink, the kiddie one. That's where he went, to the clean sink, with a smile: I'll use the one you cleaned because you did such a good job.

A look back: That's the kiddie sink.

Okay, so maybe the janitor guy doesn't understand, it's the gesture that counts.

He washed his hands and then leaned way down to wash his face. When he straightened up, there was a face stuck in his face. It was the janitor guy's.

"What about the children?" the janitor guy said. "Where will they go? Where will they go to wash?"

He smiled at the janitor guy. "I don't know," he said.

He didn't know.

He didn't know about the little children. **Q**

The Inquiry

It made him jump. It was one of those things you just barely see out of the corner of your eye—you see it just for a millimilli second and you're not sure what it is. It could be anything, including a giant rock coming at your head at a million miles an hour. That's what makes you jump. That's what made him jump when he was driving his car.

So at first all he did was jump and the car swerved a little, but luckily he was the only one on the road. He saw it out of the corner of his eye, moving fast like a ball, no, like an animal, coming right for the car. No, it was like a dog chasing after the tires, except that it wasn't barking. But it was big and scary. Then he was really scared, because it was a cat.

He was coming up to a stop sign, so he was slowing down. And it was a stop sign, so he couldn't speed up and get out of there fast. He had his window open and he was sure, he was absolutely sure that it was going to jump up and come in through his window, hissing, spitting, making ferocious noises, and looking like some catlike kind of devil. He'd never seen a cat move so quick. It was wiggling like furry Jell-O. And he knew it was going to come in through his window and scratch his face off. His forehead got hot and he felt like he was going to faint. It would dig into his eyes. It would eat his brain. He saw himself crawling into the emergency room and writing on a piece of paper: *A cat scratched my face off.*

Life, he thought, is a cruel and unusual thing.

The cat was under the car now. Or had it gone into that garbage over there? No, it was clinging to the chassis of the car, and it was getting ready to jump in.

He sped away from the stop sign, sweating and shaking. He had hardly come to a complete stop.

He looked back, but he didn't see anything. Where had it

gone? Then he knew. It had somehow got in and was behind the seat, claws and teeth ready to go. It was like a cat, only made by the devil.

He pulled over and got out. He stood there and nobody was anywhere on the road. He was all alone with his car with a cat in it. He looked in through the back windows. He saw the back seat. It had a jump rope and a bottle of Pepsi and a pocket dictionary. He didn't see the cat, but he could feel the cat. He knew it was there.

This is not fair, he thought. Why did it pick my car? Why aren't there people to help me? He peeked under the car. Dirt, metal, tar.

The cat is on my back! he thought. He scrambled out from under the car with his head still under the car and cut his neck up. He was reaching and swatting his back where he could get at it. He felt the back of his head, which had some blood on it. It was running down his back. What an idiot I am, he thought, and he would have laughed, but his head hurt too much. He checked under the seats.

He drove to the drugstore. He went in and got some Band-Aids and a bottle of aspirin. He looked at the magazines, but there was nothing interesting. Nothing at all about cats or devils. When he got to the counter, the girl smiled at him.

"Will that be it?" she said.

He nodded. "Do you live around here?" he said.

She waited a moment and then said, "Mm-hm."

He said, "Has anything strange been happening?" And he looked around to see if anyone was there. "Like have you heard in the news or from friends? I mean, anything about animals? That they've been killing people or anything like that?" He shrugged, looked around. "You know, cats maybe."

"I'll have to ask the manager," the girl said, and went to the back of the store.

Ah, the manager will know, he thought. **Q**

Wax Paper

Last night I thought of wax paper. Actually, maybe I dreamed it, sat upright in bed and thought of wax paper. I thought, where is it, what has become of it? What a great thing it was.

Someone thought of a wet fish and invented wax paper. What a good person. Wax paper was a concept, an idea.

I remember three kinds of sandwiches. Peanut butter and jelly, bologna with mayonnaise, tuna fish. Those were my three sandwiches, they were all I ate. No cheese, no lettuce, no tomato.

I never traded sandwiches. A sandwich was made by my mom. She got up early and made it for me because she loved me. To give it away would be like saying, Thanks for the love, but I've got this over here.

I gave my apple away a lot.

Wax paper I don't remember enough about. Maybe it was because of Baggies. Baggies Alligator Bags with Twisties. But I remember Paul Reilly and Ralph Scalise both had wax paper. Why? Baggies were newer, Baggies were better. They would keep what Mom made out of love tasting better. Much more like Mom had wanted it to be.

Oh yeah, egg salad, too. My mom would say, "You have to have Baggies for egg salad. Wax paper couldn't hold a candle to Baggies with egg salad."

But, still, wax paper. It was always in the house. My mom would use it for pies, for some reason I can't remember. Line the pie plate or something. And for something to do with cookies. I remember her saying, "Okay, get out the wax paper." And I knew right where the wax paper was. First drawer, silverware. Second drawer, bread. Third drawer, tin-foil, Baggies Alligator Bags, and wax paper.

It makes me want to go back there. Not to say hi, not to see how things are, but to sneak in (I have a key) and check that third drawer and see if wax paper is still there.

See how it's doing. **Q**

COOPER ESTEBAN

Ontological

On the bluffs of Hell
men with big dicks stand
in knee-high grass wait-
ing to piss. The cool
diurnal breeze licks
their immortal balls,
which have retreated
for warmth, drawing in
the tiny scrota
tighter than melons.
Hours, days, eons
ago, these same men
more than drank their fill
in Hell's cabana,
then wandered toward this
overlook—no buzz
on, no smeary sight,
no shrilly swollen
bladder—aching for
relief. On the bluffs
of Hell, sober men
stand with fingers curled
around their dicks, wait-
ing, wanting to piss.

*for Denis Johnson—because I took
the first line from him*

Paracelsus

I journeyed to the seventh sky,
so far beyond our world
that Christ had given up the throne
and shed his purple robe

to wander in that paradise
of fruits and nuzzling beasts
as naked as the newborn man
whom God bent down to kiss.

He showed his hands, deprived of wounds,
his smooth and virgin side,
and offered me a vision of
the metempsychotic self.

I heard his call, but could not quit
his globe, his whirling firmament.

Jung's Dream

I built a graveyard on the beach
    with sand and weathered rocks;
from jagged shell-scraps, lined with moss,
I fashioned the archetypal couch.

I laid to rest a swollen fish
    whose eyes a gull had torn,
whose rigid heart I clearly saw,
although the bones still held their flesh.

But when I raised a narrow dike
    to block the rising tide,
the dead savant forsook his bed
and ordered me to speak his name.

I woke and wrote of this to Freud—
and that my cock was limp and cold.

Cain't

My mama—a little barefoot girl at
play in the damp silage of a two-bit
dairy farm north of Irving, Texas—grew
up with her mama's Georgia in her mouth.
On Saturday nights she waited with the
brothers for her turn in the number 10
warshtub Aint Fay tended in the co'ner
of the kitchen after she boiled kettles
of rotten egg water. That lye soap liked
to kilt 'em, and Aint Fay's mean way with a
scrubbing sponge.
        Dirty little kids come to
my door, day in and day out, selling peanut brittle, concentrated cleaner, fresh
plums. I want to tell them no, but I cain't.

The Eunuch's Apology

The soldiers called me "faggot-boy"
and sprayed their semen in my curls,
or spread my legs as if to kiss
    my nonexistent balls.

They whistled when I passed the ranks
    and threatened to explore
the womb they wagered up my ass
with the heated point of a spear.

Now they decay in common graves,
    unmourned by bastard sons
and helpless to assault the men
who rape and slave their pretty ones.

But I have severed Caesar's head
and slept at Alexander's side.

Hunting the Rust Belt

We eat what deer eat. Smoke
wags from black stacks
overhead, an acre of earth

the price for an ounce
of pure ore. Scattered among husks,
the backbones of a buck

lie like loose change.
Hounds run wildly downwind
through fields of corn

bleached by rain.
This season, hunters grow
thick in the woods.

Even the trees pull triggers.

Empty Street

Remember the night we both woke at once
as at a signal and, turning to each
other without a word, wrung our bodies
together with the hunger of souls
seeking the flesh so lately lost to death?
And after our silent struggle, as we
lay resigned to the finality
of total dark, remember how we heard
outside the slow passing of horses
and iron-rimmed wheels, but when I cracked
the window blind to look, the brick street
was empty? What country had we entered
in that notch of grief, what miracle
or tragedy of sleep and dream showed us
the way to sunrise once again,
and where have we traveled since?

The Suicide

She hanged herself.
The day was repetitious,
No different than the rest:
Packed their lunch,
Turned the children out.
Drank our coffees separately,
One with cream, one without.
Asked between the news and me
If we could talk some more.
Saw the bitch about to mess
So led her to the door.
Began to say, but then she stopped
As I rearranged my tie.
Kissed me off at 8:00 A.M.,
And I returned the lie.
Then smeared in brightest red
—that's all—with lipstick
Across our bedroom mirror
And my startled face.
Then hanged herself.
Just hanged herself, that's all.

The Ram's Head

I saw the Venus of Willendorf's daughter
Last Saturday night at the Ram's Head,
Her sleek tanned body a coil of moist clay
Ready for itinerant artists to mold it right.
Between the jukebox and intoxicated shouts
We raised our beers and whistled unholy lusts.
Without a trace of scorn, the troubling torches
Of her eyes rekindled dim chambers of the mind,
Wondrously drawn, where chanting men
Worshipped monstrous breasts and thighs
By wielding anointed mammoth tusks.

The Magnum Opus

The King had inquired about the progress of the Magnum Opus. I sent back word of my investigation into the variance of hue between the color on the upper side and the color on the bottom side of a mulberry leaf teetering in the least of evening breezes.

The Good Dream

My mind is daylight dancing off water.
Swallows blotch the heart's back wall.

Other lives are breaking in.
The dead are everywhere.

The Flesh

In Proust's great work *In Search of Wasted Time*,
there is a wonderful girl named Albertine,
whose fruitlike breasts Proust often wants to fondle.
He contemplates the clothing of Albertine,
containing Albertine and her little breasts.
He has in mind the ultimate Paradise
of dozens of naked Albertines on a beach,
their dewy bodies glinting in morning light.

That Albertine was a man whom Proust adored,
who wrecked his plane in the Atlantic Ocean,
is certainly a fact worth mentioning.
This vision of Albertine in her chemise
can blossom forth to fill the mind with flesh
becoming spirit, which is a great thing,
whoever he or she may in fact have been
in time or out of time, in a cloak of skin.

To His Beloved, Any Beloved

love me because
I am a cripple
and dying
to drool
all over
you

love me because
my mom didn't
tit me
so I need yours
to suck
off
of

love me because
you look like
you are the only
one
blind
enough

love me because
I will love you
then
will
fuck you

Two Almost of a Kind

Next to him
who trips
and twists
100 times
more than
I do
see everyone's
almost
too busy
sticking their
eyes out
at him
to look
at me
but
I don't get
too close
to him
I can't take
the look
of him
it's too much

Cat

I got to kill
the only pussy
I got
because it's
trying to
fool me
lying
all spread out
shoving against
my face
but I'm not
fooled
it's not
the pussy
I need
and I can't
take it

An Interrogative Sentence

Can anyone
tell
that this part
works
that out of these
shaky ones
there's one
that's shaky
a lot
like the others
except this one
works
like anyone's
if only
I could
get to
just show
this one
to someone

The Night Granddad Showed Up

Yes, if you wait long enough
the similarities
of blood become apparent
as my grandmother
who floated child to child
starting with my mother
until my father died
one Christmas night
her husband—surprise appearance
(I don't know him)—
comes out of the snow
white hair huge frame
and red face looking
Irish to say hello
to which all
the relatives said no
but I Jeanne d'Arc
in my child's mind
thinking love
say yes let him go
upstairs to see Mary
so they felt ashamed
not to
and stood around
at the bottom
waiting for something
like an epiphany
when she appeared
frail as wire
not unloving says
get him out of here

and then there was
a tumult
as in some Irish bar
where the bouncers
take charge
and I losing sainthood
am condemned to repeat
her boatless swims
often getting burned.

The Afterlife

My wife's face is the color of a moth.
Soon she will be sitting in the next room
with a stranger who will hypnotize her.
Her dreams will pour forth like scarves
in a stiff breeze and gather
into a seamless garment, one the doctor
wears; one that says, you're cured;
you can go home now, lead
a normal life.

When we leave, it is cold.
The air is indistinguishable
from the invisible sunlight.
We are naked. We have grown
wings. The past is far away.
From a distance it seems
peaceful here. We begin
to fly. Nothing can stop
what happens next.

ED ADAMS

Lily of the Valley

Well, it's fun so far, she's pleased

sky's up, ground's down, and a bush,
wacky with wind, beside us

it's conveyed,
to the head

        cracked white cloud
        she crouches under

        to eye and smell
        delicate white bells

        and not look upon her, stone
        desire

Will she,
having been abused by another's
disturbed power, crush
this fragrant
flower, proffered through the same spirit,

or permit it
to wither under
a May sun

the buildings, those stern tents
will molder
all's transformed of passion, or base want
of reward

O that her pleasure taken
in the pinched odor
of so tiny a flower
would heal
the head

but I'd build again a floor

ceiling and walls and leave
the reverberating bush outdoors
for she is pleased

for Louise Bogan

Die —

© 89

[1]

San Francisco. Spring 1988.

Idle chat around the AIDS hotline. On Thursday afternoons I'm the only uninfected person, the only one not on AZT. Somebody says, "All these people are killing themselves," and names a man who used to work on the switchboard. Mention is made of the Hemlock Society. Someone says, "I know how to do it. Thirty seconal and a bag over your head." I say I thought you had to have curare or something to keep you from vomiting. "I mean, vomiting into a bag, yuck."

Ed listens to a caller and asks, "Has anybody heard of an AIDS hotel?" I say, "Sounds like a roach motel."

"A theme park," someone says. "One of San Francisco's attractions."

Last December.

Jack's ashes came in a brown plastic container the size of a shoebox. The man handed me an envelope and said, "This is your permit." I looked at him and said, "Permit to do what?" He said, "It's like those tags on your pillow. They have to be there but nobody ever checks."

The container was heavy; I walked along talking to it, sort of stroking it, "Okay, babe. We'll be okay. We can do this."

Jenny and I scattered the ashes at Port Costa. Cold stormy day, fierce winds, power failures all over the East Bay. I slipped on the rocks and sat down hard and cut my hand and got up and emptied the ashes in the spray. Some blew back on my pants. Two fishermen on the beach, watching. In the bar afterwards we'd just ordered drinks when the lights went out.

I rent *Hot Truckin'*, a porno made at least ten years ago. Before the credits I recognize a performer who I didn't know was in the cast. He's billed as "Larry le Blanc," and his character is named "Nick Rodgers." In this film he's young, bearded, with almost a full head of hair, playing the trucker buddy of the lead stud; a pal, not one of the submissive conquests. Later in his career (now billed as Nick Rodgers), after a few movies as a top, he shaved the beard, lost most of the hair, and mainly got fucked.

Last year *Variety* ran an obit of Larry White, dead of AIDS, early thirties, a Las Vegas costume designer also known for his work in adult films as "Nick Rodgers."

Watching the movie is strange, with a bit of the feeling of an old Harlow film, or something with Lupe Velez, in which the fate of the performer is superimposed on the story, giving it a slight morbid charge. In movies of the thirties, of course, you figure most of the actors are now dead, along with the era they inhabited. Which is also true of *Hot Truckin'*.

This subtext doesn't, of course, prevent me from jerking off while watching.

I answer the phone for various AIDS organizations around town. The Foundation, Catholic Charities, Project Inform. It's my niche.

Mainly I'm a subsistence rentier, and my part-time activities don't tax me much; I blend into all the guys on disability (or GA or SSA or something else that kicks in with a diagnosis), making the same rounds. I don't lie, but I keep pretty quiet about not having it.

It sometimes occurs to me that I could pack it in, all this AIDS stuff. Cut back, anyway. Cut way back.

He was scared when they told him he might have toxo. "Some of those guys," he said, "they get real crazy." I didn't know what he meant.

Actually, it was PML. Toward the end they tied him down; he was forever twitching, trying to sit up, robotic. I followed him around, holding on to a sort of leash, up and down the corridors, into empty rooms; once he peed on a night table before I could stop him. I thought of him as Jack Egg, wanted it to be over.

"What will you do," Jenny said, "when he dies?" (Or, as the social worker put it, "May I ask you a personal question? How's your support system?")

The Foundation holds a fancy fund-raising dinner (a hundred dollars a plate) honoring four leaders, including ("posthumously") Jack. The program says, "Accepting the award on his behalf will be his longtime friend," me. They present me with an inscribed crystal vase. Looking out at the Galleria, I can see only the lights in my face, hear only the microphone reverb. I begin by saying, "I feel kind of strange being up here tonight, standing in for the ghost at the banquet." I mention "mixed feelings," thank the appropriate parties, and get off.

On the whole, a pleasant evening.

There are people who keep body counts of their losses in the epidemic. The totals are often quite precise: sixty-three, or eighty-seven, or whatever. Entire social circles, I guess; lovers, tricks, brothers, cousins, neighbors, co-workers, landlords, fourth-grade teachers.

Me only (A. Tennyson, op cit) cruel immortality consumes.

Saturday on Clement. A blond boy in a baseball cap, jeans, T-shirt, sits on the sidewalk in the sun, back against a storefront, legs apart, barefoot, yawning, occasionally scratching his ankle. I go past him three or four times, till I run out of pretexts.

Memory and desire.

The first night in Garden-Sullivan Jack shared a tiny room with a very sick man behind a curtain; loud, rasping

noises. An old woman in a gray coat in the doorway, occasionally inching into the room, trying to see around the
curtain.

About a month later, a call on the hotline: a woman whose
son had recently died. "My son hated me," she said; he
wouldn't see her even at the end, wouldn't let her into his
room. I mentioned I had a friend in the hospital, and she asked
which one, and when I told her she asked if I was short and
had dark hair and if my friend was blond.

I said I was sorry about her son and she said she'd pray for
Jack. We talked a while and it was hard to end the call; "God
bless you," she said.

According to Derek, the AIDS Foundation has a
"three-year plan" for expansion of services. The hotline, he
says, now has more people than the whole foundation had
when he started. (Lots of career "public-health" types now.)
It's like Vietnam, with a minority of combatants and masses of
support troops.

Project Inform runs a hotline and distributes fact
sheets on experimental drugs.

At the training Patrick says, "I'm not interested in tunnels
full of white light and people greeting me from the other
side." He also says, "Confusion is the correct deduction from
the existing information."

As part of training, I listen to Barry handle a caller who
keeps asking, "But what should I do? What do you think?"
Barry won't be drawn in and later says, "I left him un-
happy. But I can't tell him what to do. If I knew, I'd be
doing it."

Last fall they told Jack Roberto was dying. Jack went
to the hospital every day, gave him his crucifix. "This," he said,
"is going to be a hard one."

Roberto got better. He would come to Garden-Sullivan, and go on feeding Jack ("Just another bite, darling") after the rest of us gave up.

Soon he's going back to Paraguay, to his family. "Probably I'll die," he says. One night he gives me a sport coat and two glass cups, to go (it occurs to me) with the stuff from Jack, and Mother, and Michael. Clothes, knickknacks, stuffed animals: the belongings of dead people.

At Catholic Charities there's some guy in the lobby with a shopping cart full of clothes and stuff; thin, ragged, with purple spots on his neck. I tell Bob as I come in; "Must be one of ours," he says.

The AIDS/ARC program deals with poor, often homeless people, needle users and drinkers drifting between cheap Tenderloin hotels. (And, more and more, the fallen middle class—including, one day, the former head of another AIDS agency, now sick and facing eviction.) There's emergency money for rent, medicines, and things like one-way tickets home to families.

They've been conned a lot; plane tickets sold to buy dope, that kind of thing. One time I talk with a man who says his social security check's been stolen. He's very upset: "I knew this guy, I was in PWA groups with him," he says. "I mean, who do you trust?" He says it's all he can do to get to the hospital and back, and starts to cry. "How much can I take?" A few days later a social worker calls to warn us about this same guy, who he's heard is "double-dipping" (getting money under different names).

Among my volunteer duties is closing files when clients die. The name is marked over in red with a felt-tip pen, and the folder is stapled shut.

I listen, in the evening, to the Gregorian chant requiem mass. "The traditional liturgy of the dead," the notes say, "is not only the most appropriate prayer possible for their souls, it is also an incomparable source of consolation for the family and friends who mourn them. It contains no dismal sadness or enervating sentimentality."

The assumptions, the rituals, the world are gone and forgotten. The music survives, as in stone chapels centuries ago in an age of disease and faith.

Hotline.

He's late twenties, from a little town in the Valley. He's still high on coke after driving back from San Francisco. He owes money to dealers there. "They knew I was bi," he says, "and that's why they thought of me." To get drugs, he had to let a lot of guys fuck him. No condoms. "I was just lying there. All night. I just got back. I'm real sore. A lot of these guys are needle-users. They were taking pictures. They said it's hard to get guys to do these movies now." (He tested negative six months ago; I tell him to wait eight weeks before testing again, there's no way to know about his prospects.) He keeps saying, "It's wearing off. Anymore, it hardly lasts an hour or two." He says he couldn't talk about this without the coke. "It's only been bad the last year." He's lost his wife, his daughters, his house. Still has his job (he works "for the government"; "Probably an air traffic controller," I tell Eric later).

Between asking about drug programs, he says, "I'm coming down. Oh, Jesus, I need more." And then: "I'm afraid I'll have to do it again."

(When he hears, Eric—who has AIDS—says, "Oh, God, that's my fantasy." And I admit, I'd like to see the movie.)

We were an odd match, Jack and I. When he was dying and I was cast as next of kin, I felt there ought to be somebody better—family, lifelong friends, etc. (A romantic idea, as others pointed out; often there's nobody at all.)

That night at the flat, after Jenny left, I got very drunk and clung to him, sobbing, "I don't want to lose you, I don't want to lose you." And, out of nowhere: "I love you."

He had almost no strength by then. He said, "You're going to lose me, on this planet." Stuff like that, several times. I just howled. I said (like a child), "I *am* this planet."

He couldn't stay awake and I left.

The next morning Jenny called. "I think it's wonderful," she said, "how much you love him." I hadn't known, among other things, that it showed. I said it didn't feel wonderful, it felt stupid. (She also said, "It's time. He's being very brave.") I was scared to call him, and practiced my opening line: "It could have been worse. I could have thrown up on your bed." (Which he laughed at.)

The Chronicle reports that San Francisco has, officially, the highest concentration of AIDS in the world. Also a study predicts that half the gay men here will die in the epidemic.

One in two. Heads or tails.

Ken and I discuss strategies of disclosing or withholding one's antibody status. He's joined a therapy group and after a month or so has realized, "from various things that were said," that he's the only uninfected member. He says, "I'm so glad I didn't say anything."

I told him once, "Not having it is, in the circles we move in, a privileged state. And privilege is always resented." I told another friend (low-risk, with ARC), "I'm very much aware that I should be there and you should be here." (This sense of walls, inmates and visitors, the way Jeffrey said after getting PCP, "It feels funny being on this side.")

Terry, on the Thursday shift, has had a mysterious fever for more than a month. Blood tests, a bronchoscopy, bone-marrow biopsy ("This one," the doctor told him, "is going to hurt a little"; he limped around the day after). No diagnosis, still. "I don't know what value it has," I say to

Elaine, "that I ask him every week how he's doing, what the
doctors say, what tests he's had."

And: "This is the process: you see these people around
when they're feeling okay. And it's real rare that somebody is
here this week and dies right away. What happens is they get
sick and, unless you know them, they disappear. And after a
long time maybe you see their pictures in the paper, or somebody tells you. But more often you never hear, and don't think
about it."

For weeks Roberto has diarrhea and vomits. He loses
ten pounds, looks sallow and bony. He has cryptosporidium;
nobody knows what's causing the vomiting, or seems to care.

Finally I stir myself, get some phone numbers at General,
prepare to intercede. I go over one evening, tell him I'll need
to get his doctor's name, his exact diagnosis, a list of his
medications.

He tells me it doesn't matter, he's going to Paraguay in the
morning. I say he's too sick, there won't be doctors there. "I
just want to see my mother," he says, "even if it's only a few
days." I feel I've neglected him badly; I ask to take him to the
airport: "Please, Roberto, *please.*" He says okay.

We're walking on Lombard, to a fast-food place (he thinks
maybe he could eat some chicken). As we wait in line at the
counter, he says no, he wants to go by himself tomorrow. "I
don't want to think about what I'm leaving," he says. "It will
be very hard for me."

From my journal, when Jack was hanging on: "In
death as in love, there's no substitute for inexperience. Pu-
rity's gone, after that."

The epidemic has lasted all this decade. Generations of
fallen warriors, generations of raw recruits. Hard-case vets,
like the woman who invited me to a party last November. I said
I didn't know, Jack was so sick. The party was two weeks away

and she said, "At least two or three people there will have lost someone that day."

And flooding into the phones the new positives, the newly diagnosed, newly scared. A guy the other day who was doing a paper and said he only had one question. I said okay. He said, "How has AIDS affected the gay community?"

I met Kevin at Jack's bedside in General. Sort of plump and mild. He said he had AIDS, was on AZT, worked at the Foundation, lived with his sister (who later sometimes came with him). When I asked Jack who he was, Jack just smiled and shrugged; and Kevin always spoke of Jack in admiring and general terms ("a PWA who helped other PWAs").

But Kevin turned out to be one of the most regular visitors—often a little off-sync (bringing things like cards and books that were far beyond Jack's capacities; maintaining an upbeat tone when there was clearly no further point) but kind and willing to stay a long time.

He was ultimately in the crowd when Jack had no blood pressure and wouldn't die, when I said, "Anybody can see that we're tired and crazy and stressed-out. An idiot could see it. *Jack* can probably see it." Kevin came back when I did at 3:30 A.M. after they phoned me; we hugged each other and I took off Jack's ring and neckchain and put the other stuff in a plastic bag (when Nan and Miguel were walking the streets and she asked him if he wanted to go back and he told her, "It's too late.") He was there at the dinner I bought at Leticia's with Jack's money, when everybody drank margaritas and got loud and wild, when I sat wrapped around Allen as he sobbed and the others made plans for an impromptu trip to Mexico, and we all crowded into a cab to the disco.

But after I planned the service Kevin didn't like it. He wanted anybody who wanted to to speak and I didn't, and Nan and Miguel (also PWAs) agreed with him and Kevin wound up saying his way had been used at all the other services he'd been to, for people who were "much more famous than Jack" and I had "no right to decide anything," and I wound up in his office on the afternoon of the service, railing against the "sacred brotherhood of PWAs, who know everything and everybody else knows shit," and saying, "Jack never gave a shit about you and you know it."

I got through the service, tranquilized to the gills (Kevin didn't come), and later Nan told me, "A lot of bad feeling was created around this. *A lot.*" But people drifted off and it faded, and last month Kevin's picture was in the paper, with details about a service (to be held at MCC, like Jack's). In some ways I would have liked to go, but of course I couldn't.

An afternoon at the gym, plugging away with the muscle queens. Someone in the locker room says, "Oh, I'm not worried. I was never a bottom person." As I've said to friends, I approach the gym these days in the spirit in which I approach flossing my teeth: to slow the rate of decay.

Gerard volunteers at the AIDS/ARC Switchboard, and speaks at the hotline training as a PWA. Last time he told them that having AIDS was like being a pioneer on the unexplored American continent, which was filled with dangers and also with "wonderful things."

At the Foundation picnic in Golden Gate Park. I'm being silly, riffing about my social circle, saying it's too crowded and I'm "not taking any more offers." Gerard says, "Wait till a few of them die." This is a little startling, from him. He later says, "Oh, I would never say anything like that. But I've been listening to you."

From a statement to the Stockholm AIDS Conference, June 1988, by a doctor from the World Health Organization: "Let us remember that we are still in the early phases of a global epidemic whose first decade gives us every reason for concern about the future."

A slow day on the hotline, just me and Dan, chatting. He leafs through the *Bay Area Reporter,* says, "Nothing happened. Nobody we know died this week." He gets started on the great sex life he's had, the wild times. He's actually grinning. "Oh God," he says, "I had *so* much fun." Little pause. "Of course, I have AIDS."

"Hey," I say, "win some, lose some."

When I first thought of writing about Jack, the title I had was "Private Moments with the Dead"; but I later realized it sounded like a necrophile porno movie.

There was something in the concept I liked, reminding me maybe of the times I've spent at various graves, communing with spirits. But Jack has no grave, and seems dispersed.

There's something shocking in the way a life just ends, with business unfinished, questions unanswered, possessions scattered, memories fading: as if our lives are bloody stumps, with phantom twitchings in the amputated future. It's hard to feel it's really about anything.

"You did a lot of your grieving," my Shanti counselor said, "before he died." Grieving is a "process" now, predictable within limits. (*The Grief Recovery Handbook* is displayed in Castro bookstores.) The terminal party goes through his own, rather briefer, process.

Hotline. A caller asks about free cremation services, and we refer him to the mortuary academy, warning him it's strictly no-frills. I say to the group (mixed—two women, a couple of guys with AIDS), "If all I got for four hundred dollars was a plastic shoebox, I hate to think what you get for nothing."

"Cardboard," somebody says.

"A Safeway bag."

"Old newspapers."
Whatever.

[2]

Almost fall.

I've been around this town so long. In the late fifties (I was twelve), my parents drove up from Whittier; and the next year to sail for the Philippines, and two years later on the return. At twenty-one I spent the summer trying to come out, going to my first bars. Back for grad school at Berkeley, to the Haight when I dropped out, to Berkeley again. Etc. Decades of accumulated interference, to be tuned out.

In September I get a letter from Paraguay:

"Larry, sorry to tell you, but the day you was writing your nice letter to my dear brother Roberto he passed away. He die peaceful on July 2 at 9:20 A.M.

"Larry, I missed my brother so much. I always loved him, and always try to protected him, right now I am thinking he's still there in S.F."

I set out to lose ten pounds I've put on since Jack. Apples, yogurt, diet tv dinners. "Everybody I know," I bitch, "is always trying to gain weight." ("I want flab," Miguel said once. "I want a thirty-eight-inch waist.") But, with lapses, I stick it out.

Along in here I go through some nasty periods, one of diarrhea and constant sniffles, raging at my body; one of hating kids. In my car I cut off a young cyclist, almost knock him over; he's got the advantage of youth, I think, he doesn't need breaks from me.

Activities, events.

The AIDS quilt (which I've never seen) will be in Washington in October. I plan to go with George, who helps me make a panel for Jack. George has lymphoma, is very thin, hairless, in a red beret. In the Names Project office, at a sewing machine, we chat about various people we've known—including his lover, who died in his arms watching *Gidget Goes to Rome*. "We're all dying," he says.

Soon he cancels and we lose touch; a few days before I'm to leave I hear he's in 5-A, very sick. He's skeletal, whimpering, still game: "I am not a happy camper." I promise him photos of Washington.

Washington. White stickers with red palm prints: "THE GOVERNMENT HAS BLOOD ON ITS HANDS. ONE AIDS DEATH EVERY HALF HOUR." On buildings and signs, in phone booths, men's rooms, the Metro, all over.

Another city with memories. A few years in grade school, my parents' home for a dozen years, in college and after. Several protest marches. The usual landmarks (the quilt is at the Ellipse, between the White House and the Washington Monument); seat of empire, the great stone maze of government buildings.

Chill dawn, open field, loudspeakers, ceremonies of unfolding. A drumfire of names all day. I kneel by Jack's panel, somewhere in the middle; try going systematically, then just wander. Aside from the expected, I overhear two teenage girls, there by accident. One's explaining to the other, who looks around and says, "Wow. Morbid."

In the evening a candlelight procession to the Lincoln Memorial, snaking (it seems) for miles. In front of the White House, loud chanting and finger-pointing: "Shame! Shame! Shame!" (I last did this route just ahead of a Vietcong flag.) Candlelight on the reflecting pool, speeches, planes rising across the dark sky, knots of people afterward singing "We Shall Overcome."

I'm staying at the hostel downtown. Two guys (mid-twenties, strapping, clean-cut) sharing the room, also back from the march. They're sort of sweet and overawed. One says, "I never saw that many people do anything for a cause." They don't know anybody in the quilt, are from upstate New York, things are backward there. Puffing up a bit, I say I'm from San Francisco, made a panel for my lover (as I'm calling him now). Their only connection, the blond one says, is, "He has AIDS and I have ARC."

The next day I spend with an old friend; at the Vietnam memorial we find the name of a boy we knew when we were boys. Again the red palm print, on the stand with the name book.

Tuesday morning at the FDA. Walking over from the Metro a woman in a business suit and sneakers, who says, "You boys be careful. There's a lot of policemen with guns." Actually it's a carnival: pickets (me, etc.), chanting, a rapid-fire choreography of sit-ins and die-ins and climbing the walls with SILENCE = DEATH banners (flagpoles too), helicopters, cameras, windows full of workers looking down. I AM A PERSON WITH AIDS T-shirts; wheelchairs; the first thirty-six arrested include thirty PWAs. Palm prints on parked cars.

Another Eastern city, another old friend (from gay lib in Berkeley, early seventies). Cold day, a café on a lake. "I wish you had it," he says, "so I could talk to you on an equal level. It's like a pane of glass." He has symptoms, is on AZT; his lover is uninfected. "I tell him, you'll have the house, and you're young enough to find somebody else."

He doesn't understand the quilt; why not leukemia or something? I say it's political: *these* lives have value which has been denied. He wonders about being in it.

When I get back George is of course dead. (Anyway, I didn't take a camera.) At the hotline with Preston, who has AIDS and is a veteran since the Foundation was two phones in a room on Castro; I say George deserves a quilt panel, "But I have others to do." (I'm thinking of Roberto and of Miguel, whom I've learned about in Washington.) "Yeah," Preston says, "like me."

Despite his diagnosis, his stable health is a running joke. "Preston," I say, "you're alive, so shut up."

A dangerous AIDS-testing initiative is on the ballot, endorsed by the governor. After much procrastination I get to the campaign office, am sent to a shopping center near Novato, stand nervously outside a Lucky store, saying, "Are you planning to vote?" and handing out leaflets. One woman says, "Right on," one man says, "I hope we win;" most say nothing, or detour around me. The measure loses, however.

Project Inform has a national 800 number.
A guy in a V.A. hospital in Biloxi. "I've got pneumocystis, and I'm getting worse. I'm burning up. I'm all alone here, they won't tell me anything." Crying hard. "Oh, God. I'm gonna die."
A guy in Colorado, "middle of nowhere." Medication questions, I ask his symptoms, he says thrush and fatigue and "this virus in my eye, which has made me blind."
There's almost no paid staff, and P.I. has a lot of esprit (nearly everybody's infected, lots of AIDS/ARC). I forget sometimes, feel part of a gallant, doomed little band, like the R.A.F. But I'm separate: "The twenty-year reunion," I tell Preston, "will be me and a couple of lesbians."

Winter coming, rain. Beggars everywhere, with cardboard signs and bedrolls. "Please, sir . . ."
My relation to AIDS has gradually changed: everyone I knew through Jack is dead or gone (Nan back to Australia, another last reported in Texas) and it's just volunteer days and a few social contacts. (I've given up my Thursday hotline shift; now and again I hear about Dan or Gerard, or see them on the streets, looking thinner.)

Thanksgiving. A year exactly since Jack died. I go with Preston to the Foundation's PWA dinner in the Green Room (where I went last year with Roberto and the others, ducking out twice to call the hospital, going back there later to wait by the bed). Balloons again, entertainment, open bar, linen and silver, a feast; but the PWAs and PWARCs seem shabbier, paler. In the men's room two Latinos, headbands, cowboy hats, leather jackets. "Fuck it, man," one says. "Look man," says the other, "you don't got to die with AIDS, you got to live with AIDS."

[3]

On the Texas plains, in a convertible with tailfins. Cool morning, faint sun, radio blasting. Sunglasses, heavy coats. Dark-blue sky.

Jack hasn't died. He's driving, it's the trip we planned so long. (He'd never been east of California.) At sunrise we've left a motel in New Mexico, eaten at a truck stop, pancakes and eggs.

In the motel we've finally made love, the way we should have (but I was scared and he was sick). You can prevent it now—a pill, cheap and easy; among other things, we come in each other's asses.

It's fun to be out here, horizon in every direction, road ahead to the Gulf, Atlantic, anywhere.

"Jesus," he says, "I feel good."

"Didn't I say so? Didn't I promise?"

The music's making the car shake. Something heavy-metal, young, raw.

"Where are the cowboys?" he says. "I want cowboys."

"Slut."

"Yup."

"We want cowboys!" we yell. "We want cowboys!"

Streaking down the road, nobody but us. **Q**

So you don't get confused, here is a list of people who are going to pop up:

Tom. . . . Debbie Russo's brother. Father of Marselina.
Marselina. . . . My first child.
Dick. . . . Father of my second child.
Darrin. . . . My second child.
John. . . . Possible father of Darrin.
Harry. . . . Father of my third child.
Tracy. . . . My third child.

First, you probably want to make a joke about the father's names: Tom, Dick and Harry, but I am asking you nicely, don't. Second, the background on this begins with my mother, a single parent, who, when my father left for good, broke every dish in the house and then chased him down the street for three blocks, carrying the kitchen mirror that was over the bathtub and then threw it in the middle of First Avenue when he jumped on a bus. Then she came home and put everything back together with my brother's airplane glue.

"That's one big mouth less to feed," my mother said.

The dishes ended up being a waste of glue because you had to eat your cereal fast to get any milk and because of the floor being sticky all the time.

Everyone complained about that.

My next topic, what we then called getting "knocked up," marked the beginning of me being an unwed mother. I'm fourteen and staying over at Debbie Russo's, drinking beer and watching "The Twilight Zone," that one about when the earth gets out of control and heads toward the sun and everything plastic melts including the radio and then the earth misses the sun and everything gets cold and the melted things have icicles on them when Debbie Russo's brother insisted I go back to his room to see his record player and he put on the Righteous Brothers' "You've Lost That Lovin' Feeling," and then he told me to take my clothes off and lay down on the floor. I said, "No way," and he said, "Only kidding," and then he did this Bill Cosby ice-cream routine and I did a Smothers' Brothers' joke and then we made a tent over the bed and pretended we were in a space ship. I got to be Flash Gordon and I let him be my co-pilot and we went to another galaxy where we lost the ability to talk and then we wrestled and tickled each other and then he pulled down my shorts and we did it.

One very lucky thing is that Tom had a small dick, which I hesitate to bring up in case this falls into the wrong hands since everyone knows you should never tell a guy he has a small dick and which may seem off the subject unless you think about it, since maybe this fact contributed greatly to how I became a single parent, which is the theme of this.

About the time the garment factory moved to Brooklyn, I became a single parent. All these hippies moved into the neighborhood and I met one, Dick, in Tompkins Square Park, and he said calling myself an unwed mother was uncool. Dick had long blond hair and wore suede fringe boots like an Indian and he took me to his place on First Avenue where the McDonald's is now and where he lived with other people who looked just like him. He showed me his corner where he had a mattress on the floor and Indian print cloths hanging all around and he lit a candle that had sand on it and we smoked what he called a joint. He explained to me all about unconditional love, the collective unconscious, pacifism, Being Here Now, and then we did it.

I moved in right away. Morning has broken, we are stardust, we are golden, may the circle be unbroken, we sang. We all sat in a big circle every night and became one. It was a new age, and I didn't want it ever to end. There were fifteen of us in the apartment. Hundreds in the street. Dick said I was far out and we kissed with windowpane on our tongues. I felt the earth move under my feet.

I grew my bangs out, stopped putting eyeliner on, wore bell bottoms, and carried Marselina in an army knapsack with holes cut in it for her legs.

"You look like a vagabond," my mother said to me after her work one day.

"Mama, the word is hippy. I look like a hippy."

"Like those vagabonds who eat out of the garbage and sleep on the street. Linda, that's what you look like."

"We have a generation gap, Mama," I said, "I can't talk to you now. It's normal."

"It's normal? A daughter throwing mud in her mother's face? A daughter who looks like a hipster?"

"Hippy, Mama," I said.

I had Darrin on a mattress in the middle of the floor and my new family all held hands in a circle around me. Darrin was our first child and we would have other children, children of the universe, who wouldn't be torn by strife and we would teach them well and feed them on our dreams.

First Dick went off with Renée, who was from France and wanted to go west across America. Just before he left, he said, "You and I are soulmates, spiritually, mentally, and physically. The whole kit and kaboodle. We're like this," and he held up two fingers like they were cemented together, but

I guess he meant it in a higher consciousness realm because I never saw him again. The others went off to India or back to college. I went back to Mama's on 11th between B and C.

"What happened to the hippsies?" Mama said.

"They left, Mama," I said.

"Now look what we got. The pushers of drugs on the streets. The hippsies weren't so bad compared to this."

"Hippies, Mama."

"This neighborhood is like that other word you call yourself: a mother without a husband."

"Single parent, Mama."

"That's it. This neighborhood is like a single parent. Deserted."

Then the Japanese men bought the garment factory and things got hard at work because they didn't speak Italian and they raised the quotas.

"See what I mean?" Mama said. "The whole world is like a solitary mother."

"I don't get it, Mama."

"Linda use you noogin," Mama said, putting two fingers against her temples and then out in the air like a bird's beak. "A mother alone has to fight, fight, fight all the time. That's what I mean." She poked me in the arm with the beak.

"Times have changed, Mama," I said.

"You're telling me something new?"

The way I got my third child shows just how much times had changed. Harry, who worked at the crackhouse on the corner, brought Tracy up one day and asked would I keep an eye on her for a couple of hours, and I said, "Okay, Harry, no problem. But that's two hours on the dot, no monkey business."

"I'll be back. You have my word," Harry said, and then he gave Tracy a kiss and kept standing at the door looking at her like it was killing him to leave but something at the door was tugging him and then he came back and gave Tracy another kiss and he touched her face and then he put both his hands up in the air and said, "I'll be right back. Promise." and he made an X on his heart. Then he opened the door like he was afraid it would make noise and he tiptoed out into the hall and, as far as anybody knows, disappeared, completely disappeared, off the face of the earth.

He left a full box of Pampers.

Which, as I explained to Mama, is more than any of the other kids' fathers ever did give me. **Q**

The last time I saw my father's brother, Jerry, was the night before the seventh game of the 1955 World Series. I was thirteen. Uncle Jerry had stopped to visit us in our Wisconsin Street duplex in Rochester on his way to a beer distributors' convention in Buffalo.

I always enjoyed Uncle Jerry's visits, but my father didn't. Maybe it was because my father, who taught history at East High School, couldn't afford the kind of expensive gifts that Uncle Jerry always brought us. That afternoon, when he had arrived, Uncle Jerry gave my mother, whom he always called "Princess," a gold brooch studded with small rubies. Then he gave me a gaudy leather jacket with lots of extra zippers. For my father he had a camel's hair topcoat, which looked sharp on my father and which, I knew as soon as he tried it on, he would put away in a closet and forget.

My mother, father, and I usually ate dinner in the kitchen, but that night, as we did whenever Uncle Jerry visited, we moved into the cramped dining room, where the wallpaper was brown and covered with small pink splotches that someone must have originally intended to look like roses. I sat with my back to the kitchen. Uncle Jerry, tan and healthy-looking and wearing a blue blazer and gray slacks which somehow appeared freshly pressed after his drive from New York, took his seat across from me. In the corner to his right was the glass-doored cabinet where my mother kept her good dishes. My mother, wearing the blue dress she wore only for company, sat to my right at the end of the table. My father sat across from my mother. His steel-rimmed spectacles, thinning hair, and rumpled suit, which was brown and almost matched the brown of the wallpaper, made him look like the older brother, although Uncle Jerry was older by almost two years. On the sideboard behind my father was a small Seth Thomas clock, which he and my mother had received as a wedding present. When I had been much younger, I had moved the hands of the clock forward in order to hear the chimes ring or to try to make Howdy Doody time come sooner. As a result of my tampering with time, the clock always ran slow.

As my mother ladled out bowls of stew, Uncle Jerry recounted how, the previous October, the New York Giants had exposed the Cleveland Indians for the imposters they were. Then he went on at some length, using language which, had I used it, would have earned me at least a month in my room, about what the Yankees were going to do to the Brooklyn Dodgers.

I knew what was coming next—what always came next—and I was embarrassed for Uncle Jerry, which was silly. If I had learned one thing from Uncle Jerry's stories, it was that he could take care of himself. My father took off his spectacles and, as he polished them with his handkerchief, made his customary speech that "rough language" wasn't appropriate for the dinner table. Uncle Jerry replied that the way he'd had to use his fists and sometimes other things to keep the mob from muscling in on his beer distributorship in New York had sure as hell earned him the right to use a little rough language.

My father didn't like to hear stories about run-ins with the mob, although I thought such tales were the best parts of Uncle Jerry's visits, and I always found it difficult to believe that he and my father were brothers. As my father and Uncle Jerry continued to argue, I took a long drink of water from my red-rimmed goblet, one of a set of four which my mother had inherited from her mother, and which were never used unless we had a guest for dinner. Then, with my finger, I traced the pattern of the gold decoration on the red rim until my mother had served us each a bowl of stew and my father said grace.

We ate dinner in silence, except for Uncle Jerry's requests for bread and more stew. The dining room seemed even more cramped than usual. Then my father astounded me by saying that he thought the Brooklyn Dodgers could win the game the next day because he'd heard that Johnny Podres was an up-and-coming pitcher. When Uncle Jerry dryly remarked that he hadn't known my father was a baseball fan, my father replied that he had decided to start taking an interest in sports so that he could establish a better rapport with his students.

Uncle Jerry and I looked at each other. My father was always trying some new gimmick to establish a better rapport with his students, many of whom never failed to mention, when they saw me between classes, or at Fenton's Rexall Drugstore, or on the high-school baseball field, that my father was the dullest teacher any of them had ever had.

After dinner, Uncle Jerry asked if I wanted to go for a ride in his car and maybe get some ice cream. I got up so fast I knocked over my chair. I set it upright and looked at my father, but all he said was that I could go after I had finished helping my mother clear the table and do the dishes.

I liked ice cream well enough, but Uncle Jerry knew I would have gone with him to watch a stop sign rust if it meant getting to ride in his car. He bought a new car every year and always had the latest, snappiest model. The one he'd pulled into our driveway that afternoon was a red and white '56 Thunderbird loaded with extras. I and a dozen others in the neighborhood had spent a half hour before dinner ogling the car. The paint job was so slick I was sure the car could glow in the dark. Inside, the dashboard looked better than anything I had ever seen in Saturday-morning reruns of *Flash Gordon,* and the seats were of a red leather that gave off a wonderfully rich smell, so different from the mildew smell of my father's '49 Plymouth coupé.

When Uncle Jerry and I went out the front door that night, a lot of my neighborhood friends were still clustered around the car. I eased past them and let myself sink into the softness of the passenger seat. Uncle Jerry got in, started the engine, and backed the Thunderbird out of the driveway. He drove up Wisconsin Street slowly, and winked at me again. He understood that I wanted any other neighbors who were out in the twilight to be able to recognize me in the car.

Uncle Jerry turned right onto Main Street and we went faster, but not much faster, as people in front of Benson's Grocery and Pofahl's Garage and Grogan's Bar and Grill stopped and stared, and it was the same all the way to Melrose's Ice Cream Parlor, where, inside at a corner booth, the chocolate marshmallow ice cream never tasted better.

It was almost dark when we left Melrose's. The car had attracted another crowd in Melrose's parking lot. More than a few of the onlookers were the same ones who always complained to me of how boring my father was. Now I could feel them look at me differently.

Uncle Jerry and I got in the car and headed back down Main Street. Uncle Jerry wanted to show me what the engine could do, so he drove faster, and the acceleration forced me farther back into cushioned comfort. We each had our window open, and the cool night air streaming into the car felt good on my face.

When we reached Grogan's Bar and Grill, a white Cadillac pulled out in front of our headlights. Uncle Jerry braked and yelled out with what my father called "rough language," as I flew forward and almost hit my head on the dash. The white Cadillac stayed in front of us for several blocks. The Thunderbird's speedometer showed fifteen miles an hour.

The Cadillac stopped for a red light in front of Benson's Grocery. When the light turned green, the Cadillac didn't move. Uncle Jerry shouted out more rough language and gave the horn a long, vicious blast. Two men in black suits, built like linebackers, got out from either side of the Cadillac and walked back toward us. When they reached us, the man on Uncle Jerry's side folded his arms on the door and leaned in. The man on my side leaned in, too, so that his face was only inches from mine. He took a deep breath and let it out slowly. The garlic smell was overpowering. I turned my face away and fixed my eyes on the dashboard cigarette lighter.

"You wanted to talk to us?" the man on Uncle Jerry's side said. His voice was easy, conversational, and very low-pitched.

"Actually," Uncle Jerry said, sounding like the little kids who, with a certain amount of persuasion, regularly donated their lunch money to me, "I was just driving my nephew home and I accidentally hit the horn."

"You should be more careful," the man said. "This is a very nice car."

Uncle Jerry moaned something which might have been agreement.

I was feeling nauseated from the garlic smell. I kept my eyes on the cigarette lighter. The dashboard glowed softly.

"You should be careful when you're out in traffic with this car," the man said, and nodded to his companion.

Both men straightened up, and I heard a flicking sound. A four-inch blade, gleaming in the light from a streetlamp, magically appeared in the left hand of the man who had spoken to Uncle Jerry. As the men walked back to the Cadillac, the man with the knife kept the blade pressed down on the Thunderbird's hood, leaving a long, scar-like wound.

After the men had driven away, I waited for Uncle Jerry to say something. But he said nothing. He still didn't say anything as he drove up Wisconsin Street, or when he pulled into our driveway. And a moment later, in the front hall, when Uncle Jerry passed my father, who was still in his rumpled brown suit and just putting his spectacles back on his face, I wondered why I had never before noticed that my father was the taller of the two brothers.

My father looked even taller the next day when I got home from school to watch on television as Johnny Podres shut out the Yankees. If Uncle Jerry had any comment, I never heard it. He had left for Buffalo early that morning. **Q**

DEATH

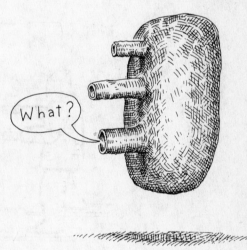

JOB

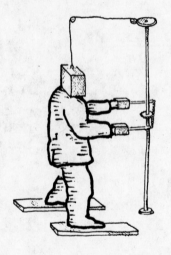

DAVID CANTWELL SCHER

Ernest
Borgnine
climbing
rocks

DAVID CANTWELL SCHER

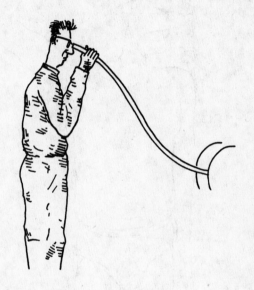

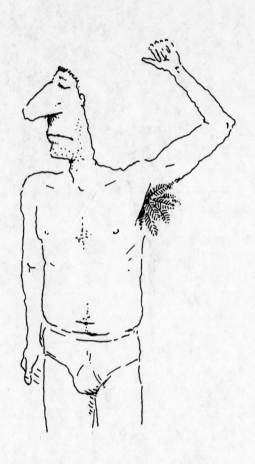

BOWL-O-BUTTS

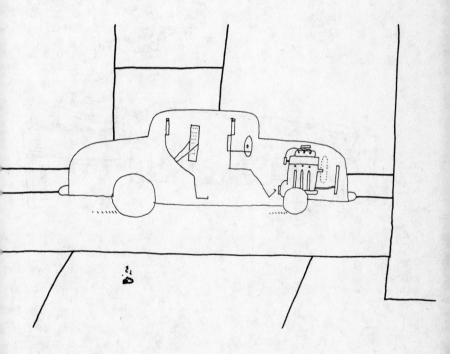

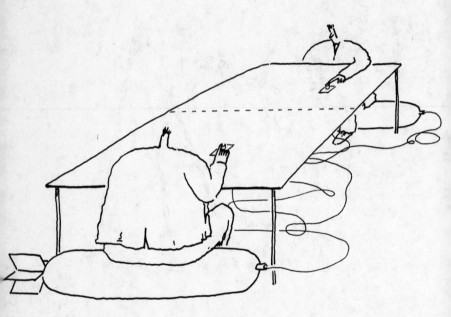

Don't know if you want to hear the gruesome details of being held in the dread back Beating-up Room of the La Ventana Dance Hall and Saloon in East Texas. It was evidently some small oversight on the part of the Blank county sheriff's department, which must have mistaken us for Bonnie and Clyde. We got thrown in there and ended up sitting for two hours with our hands handcuffed behind our backs, and having your hands detained behind your back means you have to constantly lean forward a little, or a lot, depending. And then while they are trying to decide if we are terrorists or merely unfortunate, they chucked this poor fucking cowpoke through the door of the Dread Back Beating-up Room, all bloody and fucked up, and he's bellowing "My thirty-dollar hat didn't look like that when I came in here!" And Jim looks down at this poor old boy hogtied on the floor and says, "Neither did you, son." I tell you, what that kid's face looked like was a plate of food. Mexican food. I admired him. He simply never shut up. "Cut me some slack, you fuckin' pussies, and I'll take you on one at a time!" And they'd commence beating on him again. It was sort of a tiny North American corner of the Third World, those places you dread being thrown into and losing touch with your consulate. They rifled my I.D. and came upon my press card and became suddenly cautious. Well, we were taken, still handcuffed, to some grimy Blank county sheriff's department ketchpen, and this woman, ugly as a bucket of nails, insists I sign here and pay cash for fines immediately or else, and I said, "I'm not signing that," and they didn't insist. That old useless expired press card has served me well; they'll probably bury me with the damn thing. Then they took Jim away, and all his people were waiting outside the ketchpen for him, and they sprang him, and then he came back and sprang me. All the good people you recommended for us down here were ace and endlessly helpful—and they are all very very very very sorry this happened. And so am I and Jim and Jim's Texas clan and especially the poor cowpoke with the thirty-dollar hat—that is, everybody but Sgts. Pimento and Dawson of the Blank county sheriff's department, and I would like very much for them to be sorry after I sue them for wrongful detention, kidnapping, invasion of privacy, and piracy on the high seas. Ed Paetzel located us good lawyers. They live up in high towers, and everybody can't stop apologizing for the city of Blank as if the whole city were their fault. Good people. Jim and I got to see them in city clothes; Jim takes his $300 Stetson off and l-a-y-s it carefully on the knee of his three-piece suit, his gold Rolex shines, he says Old Texas all over. And so then we went up to New Waverly by way of a town called Cut and Shoot, to the Double B Ranch. Jim's friends. Quarter-horse people. Jack Spencer. We were treated royally. Saw an awfully good deal on a two-year-old colt, nice brassy yellowjacket buckskin. No good for the track but a beautiful build for a using horse, he was compact and aggressive, saucy head, bouncy. Jim keeps saying, "The price is too high, it's too high," but he wants him. We drove around with the trainer/half-owner at feeding time and saw this colt's dam and she was pretty, but what would I do with that colt if I bought him? Where would I send him? Hey, he'll probably turn out to be the world champion cutting horse. Well, it's rank down here in East Texas with the smell of industry. Plastics plants and bayous and refineries, places called Chocolate Bayou and Seafood Depot. Jim refused to go to the city of Blank stock show until he got his Stetson cleaned at the American Hat Shop on Live Oak; he said he might run into people he knew there, and he was right, he did. Cattlemen from Missouri. And further on the hat, he said those sons-of-bitches at the La Ventana would never have laid a hand on him if he'd been wearing his Stetson, and you know what? I suspect he's right. Although he says that particular hat company has gone to hell and next time he's buying Resistol. Jim's people

took us out for barbecues and a motor ride up a bayou. Bless
their hearts, they are trying so hard to make up for us being
snatched up and insulted by the Blank county sheriff's department (I wish you could use the real county name, but I guess
The Quarterly would shit chickens), and are seeing that we enjoy
ourselves anyway. The city of Blank is full of normal people
that untoward things never happen to. Well, never mind. Rick
Bass called from Austin to offer his sympathy. There's a store
not far from here in Baytown that says THE PIG SHOP—MACE,
HANDGUNS, AMMUNITION. Tell Barbara her rose got two green
branches that survived the cold spell. Oh, yes, we went down
to the Gulf (pronounced "guff") at Galveston (pronounced
"ga-*vess*-ton") and had cold boiled shrimp (pronounced "co-
bawd srimp") and shrimp gumbo and walked out on the windy
beach and the water looked like carbonated oyster soup and
roiled and surged. The shrimp gumbo was superior. Ed Paetzel
insists the chicken-fried steak at the Confederate House is the
best in Texas, but Jim only gave it a 95. All in all, I must admit,
we have been eating our way through Texas. Jim says the best
chicken-fried steak there ever was was at the Sam Bass Café in
Round Rock, Texas, but when we went there in search of the
Sam Bass Café, two guys at the Hidalgo Barber Shop down by
the Guadalupe River said, "Shit, man, the Sam Bass Café done
burnt down three times! (pronounced tahms) Are you looking
for their people?" Round Rock has gone yuppie-arty—shops
selling Esprit and Boston Trader and a café where the men's
and women's rooms were labeled Bubba and Bubbette! The
chicken-fried steak we had there resembled a boiled boxing
glove, but, ah, the local, tawny splendors of the Guadalupe
River and the Hidalgo Barber Shop! Jim was in a fit—"This
fuckin' state, excuse my language, has gone all to FUCKIN' HELL,
excuse my language." But he was in a much better mood when
we got up to the Double B past Cut and Shoot up to New
Waverly in all those piney woods and Jack Spencer took us out
to a good Tex-Mex place and they did some damage to a bottle
of Chivas Regal and talked tort lawyers. Remember the

Alamo! Anyhow, Jim has this brother-in-law born and raised on the Galveston gulf and probably one of the world's best saltwater and bayou fishermen; he said one time he was bitten on the tit by a one-and-a-half-foot hammerhead shark while casting for redfish off a collapsing pier in a hurricane. This man would fish through World War III. Jim's sister Bobbie Ann is sweet and pretty and is showing me how to press iron-on maps of Texas onto T-shirts, and the men go out and get under pickups and discuss U-joints. When Jim first saw his nephew Tommy this time, Jim said, "When was the last time we saw one another?" And Tommy said, "I remember it was when we was pulling Eddie T.'s pickup out of the ditch! And you was shippin' that ole cow somewhere!" That ole cow was a $5,000 purebred. This city is an odd combination of bayous and piney woods and square miles of refineries. It is also the rudest and most abrasive city in Texas we've been in—people in banks, stores, etc. But *folks*—that's different. If they are your kinfolks, they'll kill for you. Anyway, off to the Deep South. **Q**

DEAR SIRS,

I am intrested in your College It is in a good location
I prefer the country and I like its smaller size It is near all my
intrest's Thier is biking and hiking and the wood's and the
feild's and also town's and bookstore's This will be my first
year I like to be sure and comfertable in my serounding's It is
vary important for me and I consider it allways.

PART 1

What is education Education means to bring forth
from the within and I wood be vary comfertable at your place
bringing me forth The individuelized program wood be perfect for me right in agreement with what Ive been doing on my
own for my life.

Some of my Experiance's I like more than other's I am
lerning an appreciation of myself and other's that is enduring
and transends personel Experiance I have lerned that Ex-
periancing full is the best for me and I dont mean just going
place's or to event's I mean doing thing's fully and watch your
own feeling's and thought's You allways try to do your best but
be avaleable to other Experiance's Really all you need is flex-
able living and be open.

I really think what many teacher's beleive above and
beyond all is that if left alone people will mess up or not lern
or grow This is not true They may not get the same answer but
for me that isnt the measure of sucksess I am not just intrested
in answer's Student's can lern in this old way but for me perso-
nelly it is really importent to show some self direcshon and
inquier on your own free will That shows that you can truely
lern but I will talk more about this later.

PART 2

You ask of a Personal Statement that tells you what I am and how I got to where I am today I was born in New Hampshir but I moved to Montana when I was small Father was in the survey business for geology I traveled with him and saw the outdoor's actualy most of this country Where Mother is Father says I Do Not Remember and Thats All I Need To Know She Is Out Of Our Life I cant say Im sad I was just too young to know Montana is the kind of place for open area's By this I mean space and not just the black sky at nite I mean the life of the open air the space to grow and wander Father wood take me on these tripp's outside over hill's and plane's camping out He had this expensive equipment and wood teach me about the sky and star's and how the cloud's move and why is the planet's brite at nite My Father lerned this way walking threw feild's and bearly going to School at all.

I did go to School partly in New Hampshir and then in Montana to the Valley Tecnical high School Thier I wood say I felt more at home with work I did less with books and more with my hands which I am more comfortable I did mostly woodshop but also skill's they taught like home finance and math and science and histery I cant say I liked the math much I rather prefered the shop It was something I was in control of Sometimes I stayed after at night and worked I guess that is extracuriculer I graduated two years ago and now work in the Factory Outlet making chair's table's and dresser's I wood say that I have some real world Experiance you talk about only getting when you get out of College so maybe Im ahead of other's in that way.

Now I am looking at a place like yours that will give me the freedom to lern By that I mean not having to take economic's or some language to lern to be a poet or metiorologist Father says Keep Your Opshons Open so I have allways explored many thing's never deciding on one thing Say I wanted to be a busnessman in the forth grade and only thawt about that all

these year's where wood I be today So I kept exploring all
subject's mostly related to nature knowing that book's in the
tradishonal sense do not intrest me What intrests me is the
larger question's not memerizing a bunch of number's to figure out a problem I want to know the reason's behind the
number's How did they know that two pie R equals the circum-
firence What is pie How did they get that number to begin with
I think most people these day's do not care about the why's but
only how to get thier faster and suckseed with the shortcut.

I lerned about your College The Alternative School in the
newspaper One of your student's is doing feild work near my
town something in Ancient Indian Buriel Grounds So I asked
him what College he went to knowing that he was doing werk
indipendant from all the teacher's and was setting his own plan
of study He said your College I said any College that wood let
me do that to is an excellant place for me but I must say now
I know nothing concerning Buriels and hope that isn't detri-
mental.

PART 3

You ask of me a project How wood I get skeptical kid's
to lern First let me say from my Experance teacher's are hard
on kid's and kid's are hard on teacher's But we are all people
so I will start by treating them that way not embearasing them
in class by calling on them when I know they arent ready.

Children and adult's are not naturally skeptical to lern
What is opporating in thier live's is that they are afrade of my
feild because they think it is above them They listen to what
I teach and think they have no base no way to get at the
knowlege So I make it new whatever my subject say metiorology so they can grasp it Student's wood be free to do as
they wish being only responsible to be productive in some way
I really beleive that people wood naturaly be sucksessfull when
they are not over whelmed and faced with pretenshus action's
behavior and word's of athority's This is a oberservashon
based from my Experance in School Say the person has no

emidiate Experiance or intrest Who am I to expect some one
to live up to some expectashon and reflect it in a test of memory No I wood take the skeptical student's and show them that
what I know I know only because of what I was brought up to
think I wood lead them to the woods near my home or the
feild's the grass I wood tell them Look up at the sky at the
cloud's See the metiorology is around us all not just some up
tight book that you have.

After I wood not be asking them to write back to me what
I just told them to tell if they lerned No I wood have them write
do project's have an experimant in the feild talk to the class
or maybe draw something about what they lerned You see they
were only skeptical in thier mind's because they did not have
the confidence to be themselve's and thought they knew nothing But if you give them a start and teach them to teach themselve's they will be better off and they will carry this with them
through life.

That is my project on teaching skeptical student's Of
course this work's for other subject's not just metiorology
Imagine the same idea's used for poetry geology histery math
chemistry or discusing great book's.

In closing I say that in my Experiance I cood have
lerned all that I got from twelve yr's of public School in three
yr's and I'm being generous Allso more harm was done than
good in my case The teacher's allways said to me I think you
have potenshal but you have to get your werk in on time I
wood allways say Sorry I need more time and they said You
have to keep up I was in class most days and the teacher's like
Mister Perrin wood say Can you tell me the atomic wait of
calcium This infermashon does not stay inside I said No I dont
know How cood I Thier is a huge table of the element's and
this or that wait makes no difference I wanted to know why
calcium has a different wait than the other's and how can I
figure it out myself But no one wood tell me and I coodnt
answer thier question's and didnt pass the test's I wood say I

spent most of my class's like this sitting and trying but not being able to remember I was really thinking more about how the star's move and why the sun sets each day a little later than before So in that sense maybe I was wasting my time Even my counseler Misses Myers said Oh I dont think you belong here Its just like Father says Those Places Never Did No Good For Me And Look At The Job I Have.

So I am convinced of your program and its merit's I know it is best for me now in my stage of life I know if I am given the chance I can really asert myself The question is can I eccept the challenge of all that space the room to lern the indipendance I think I can I hear your sky's are clear too and you had aurora borelalis last month I hope I can come to your College to see what can I make of those being's in the brite sky.

To sum it up Albert Einstine said it well Education is that which is left after everything lerned in School is forgottin.

COMMENTS:

The proverbial heart goes out to this one. On the one hand, the essay is somewhat marred by a certain uneasiness with mechanics. On the other hand, however, one can easily sympathize with much of what is expressed. Isn't it obvious the applicant can think? There are ideas about learning here which are clearly well developed, and the critique of traditional education is quite informed, articulate and sincere. Recommend that we ask candidate to visit for interview and tour, to observe some social interaction on a more relaxed and personal basis. **Q**